INSIDE THE DESIGN INDUSTRY

INSIDE THE DESIGN INDUSTRY

NAVIGATING YOUR FIRST STEPS IN COMMERCIAL ARCHITECTURE, INTERIOR DESIGN, AND ENVIRONMENTAL BRANDING

BRITTNEY HERRERA IIDA, LEED AP

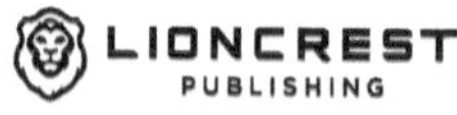

INSIDE THE DESIGN INDUSTRY

Navigating Your First Steps in Commercial Architecture, Interior Design, and Environmental Branding

FIRST EDITION

ISBN   978-1-5445-4734-3   *Hardcover*
       978-1-5445-4733-6   *Paperback*
       978-1-5445-4732-9   *Ebook*

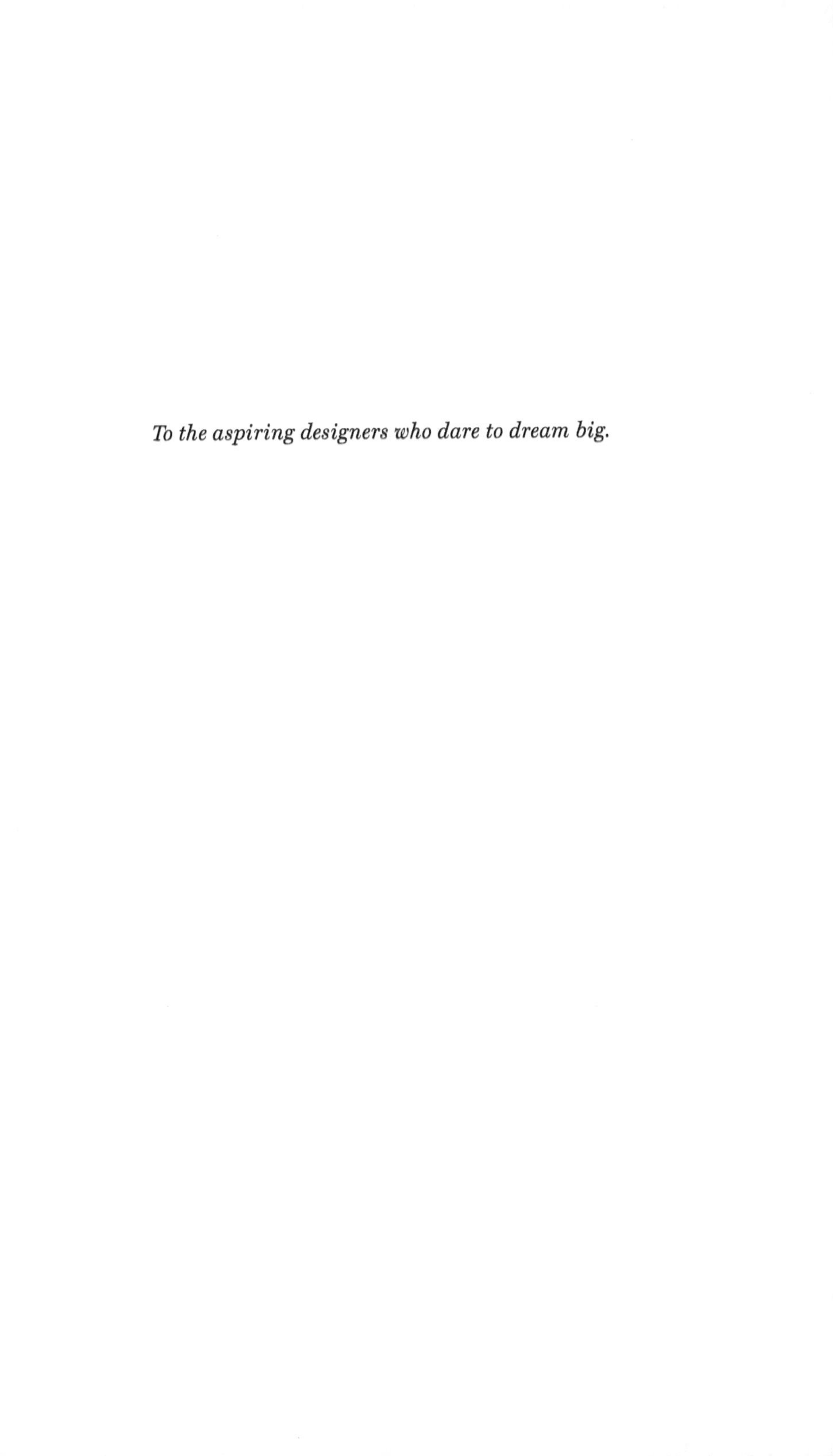

To the aspiring designers who dare to dream big.

CONTENTS

INTRODUCTION

"YOU ARE IN THE BIG LEAGUES," A SENIOR DESIGNER TOLD me, narrowing her eyes at the finish board I'd volunteered to take off her plate. "We don't do boards like this."

My breath caught, and my excitement to turn in my first official finish board at my new firm, ADD Inc, dissolved into panic. I looked down at my board and didn't know what she meant. This was supposed to be an easy project. She'd chosen to give it to me, the temp materials librarian who would happily take any job just to get her foot in the door with the design staff. This was my chance to impress.

Instead, I'd failed miserably and didn't even know why. My board wasn't in the big leagues? With one statement, all the hopes I'd pinned on this project—that I'd elevate my role from ADD's temp librarian to the newest full-time interior designer— were crushed.

But I didn't give up that easily.

Girding myself for the critique ahead, I asked, "Can you tell me what I did wrong?"

The senior designer spent the next thirty minutes picking

apart my board. My spacing was off. My alignments looked sloppy. Even the way my velcro was facing came under fire. "What if the client pulls this off the board and needs to put it back on?" she chided, demonstrating how user unfriendly the reversed velcro strips were with a pitiless *riiiip*!

Iris wasn't doing this to be mean. Her standards were high, and she didn't exempt herself from meeting them. She planned her boards out in CAD and then printed them to the size of the board to use as her cutting template. She cut every piece of velcro to the same precise dimensions with an X-Acto knife and used a label maker to mark every material neatly and clearly. My original board was nice. It was tidy. It was functional. But it was nowhere near her level.

I swallowed any modicum of pride I had left and listened to her, busily taking notes on every area of critique, every piece of advice. Then I redid the board, laying it out in CAD the way she would have. I added a title block and placed the material labels with care. To do one better, I labeled the materials in CAD, and behind each sample, I typed the material, its location, and its specification information. I laminated it to gator board and then added the velcro in two-inch lengths, facing the same way. It was better than what I'd been instructed to do.

When I brought my revised board to Iris, she looked at it carefully, inspecting it for errors. Then her face relaxed, and she gave me a slight smile. "This is the best board I've ever seen," she praised, "I expect you to do all your future boards like this."

I beamed. Iris took me under her wing and taught me everything about industry standards, the importance of options for the client to choose from, and how to arrange a presentation so clients could easily follow the pitch. She taught me how to manage things as small as task lists and as big as whole projects. She taught me the best way to file a project away, how to fold fabric memo samples, how to do a code plan, and so much more.

She was also getting her work done more quickly and efficiently with my assistance. The whole office looked in to see how I could help on their projects. Before long I was working across the firm, building a reputation for being helpful. Managing both my library workload and project responsibilities was a welcome change. It did result in a few all-nighters, but they were a badge of honor, not a burden.

One day, I overheard a design manager struggling with a space plan. She said, "No one can make this layout work—the program just doesn't fit!" Space planning was one of my superpowers and, as I would later learn, a real differentiator for me in the firm. I asked if I could take a look, and she agreed. An hour later I gave her back an efficient solution that made her speechless. She looked at me in disbelief and took the layout around to the other designers who'd given up on it. I was proud that my skills were becoming valuable and that I had done something that no one else could do. It gave me confidence that I belonged among this talented group of professionals. I remember that layout to this day.

Showing my ability to be trained and to be a team player was the real source of my success in the early days of my career. I thrived on feedback. I could make senior designers' lives and budgets easier. I understood that my time and effort impacted their ability to meet their deadlines and their project success metrics. I was now a valuable resource.

When my three-month temp position was up, I was offered a full-time position.

So how did I do it?

DESIGN IS A TEAM SPORT

Those who get into the field of designing for the built environment do so for many reasons. Perhaps you had visions of being a sole proprietor and helping people to create the homes of their dreams. Perhaps you love travel and were inspired by beautiful hotels and the layered network of event spaces, guest amenities, and retail. Or perhaps you love to create fully branded workplace experiences that support the teams who work there to do their best work while connecting with the company ethos. Regardless of your initial motivations, there is a complex and evolving network of professionals that go into making a building, an interior, and a branded experience. As you enter the field in professional practice, you will learn that creativity and technical ability will get you far, but not all the way.

What will make you stand out among your peers is your ability to communicate your ideas, accept and act on feedback, and build community. You will need to know who the players are and develop an appreciation for everyone's role in the design ecosystem in order to successfully build the kind of community that will carry you forward in your career and enable you to make an impact. Every large scale firm has architects, interior designers, graphic designers, human resources staff, administrative staff, and, of course, IT. Beyond the firm, there is a larger network of people who service the projects we design as well: contractors, real estate brokers, project managers, engineers, landscape architects, real estate attorneys, code consultants, building department plan reviewers, inspectors, and more. Then there are the clients themselves.

Every team member has their own agenda, success metrics, standards, quirks, and preferences. They built relationships with other design professionals long before you came on the scene. Understanding the human side of the business is critical to thriving. Leaving school and entering firm life can be a bit of a shock. You may wonder how you fit into the firm and how you build your talent among the ranks of talented people. You may wonder who all these people are and how they all connect.

In school, most of your work was done solo rather than as part of a team. You learned how to think outside the box by exploring abstract ideas. You developed a sense of where you excel and where you are more challenged. Your ideas and technical execution of those ideas resulted in grades.

A professor has different expectations from a boss. Your ability to synthesize your school work into a portfolio, paired with your early ability to network, results in your success or failure in landing a job. Once you are on the job, your boss will expect you to integrate into the team of design professionals on any given project, as well as to integrate into the firm culture as a whole.

When you join a top design firm, you go from being a senior at the top of your class to an intern with little to no experience. You can expect to design restrooms for the foreseeable future. This may feel like a slight, but it is actually a testament to your firm's investment in you. Restrooms are complex—requiring code knowledge; space planning abilities; coordination of mechanical, electrical, and plumbing consultants; understanding of ADA requirements; complex lighting solutions; finishes with slip-resistance; and knowledge of cleanability requirements—and you still have to think about aesthetics and fitting with the overall design themes that the team has set for the project. Lean into the task. It's a rite of passage.

Despite your junior designer or intern status, you are a valued part of the team. Your energy, enthusiasm, and fresh perspective remind more seasoned professionals why we do this and encourage creativity in the team. That is valuable. You are no longer running a sprint; you are now running a relay, and success depends on how you do your part and hand off that baton.

Every firm has its own culture, specialty, structure, path to advancement, and politics. The thing that doesn't change is that people in a top firm are focused on the success of the firm as a team. The sooner you figure out how you factor into that equation, the better for you and for them.

WHAT YOU'LL LEARN

Maybe you've just graduated from design school. You've won some accolades from your professors and university. You may have applied for a student award through your local or national professional association. Your portfolio looks great, but you're wondering: *How do I get hired?*

Or maybe you've just gotten hired at your dream job but now have no idea how to navigate the relationships inside your new firm. You're bumping up against your colleagues, boss, contractors, or clients, and that awesome project you thought you were going to get is now nowhere in sight. What just happened?

What I'm here to show you are the things not talked about in lectures that have nothing to do with design. Instead, the strategies and mindsets I explain here through the lens of my own journey from design graduate to firm rainmaker are all about people.

In essence, you'll learn how to grow and maintain your network, work with firm leaders, get along with coworkers, connect with industry professionals, and keep your values and energy intact in a tight-knit creative industry that can get a little wild.

I wrote this book to be a guide for designers just entering the field of commercial architecture, interiors, and environmental branding. It is written from my experience working for some of the most celebrated design firms in the world. I have made mistakes. I have had successes. I know what it takes to run a firm, from hiring the right teams to winning highly competitive projects for brands like Amazon, Google, TripAdvisor, Adidas, IBM, Fidelity Investments, and hundreds more.

I mentor people across the industry on negotiating their salary, dealing with challenging colleagues, dealing with challenging bosses, elevating their position at the firm, and endless other challenges they encounter in the field. This book maps out the complex network of industry relationships and details some of the most sought after advice I have given over the years. It is a guide for designers who are just entering the field and do not yet know the landscape of the interpersonal politics that connect us all.

It is my hope that you will walk away with a better idea of the players and the opportunities to build a meaningful community and be set up for stardom within your firm or as you take the next steps to striking out on your own.

WHY A BOOK

I am from Midcoast Maine, a place where there is a culture of excellent craftsmanship, resourcefulness, and grit. It is partly due to these values that I kept going in the industry. It never occurred to me to quit. Growing up, my dad had many quotes on hand for any given situation. One of his favorites was "Good things come to those who wait, as long as those who wait work their ass off while they are waiting," an adaptation of a quote from President Lincoln. At no point did Lincoln (or my dad) indicate when the wait would be over...so I kept going.

My dad is a builder. He is a jack-of-all-trades and can learn anything from a book. I didn't get that gift. I read, but I could read a book on arc welding ten times and still not pick it up until I tried it with my own hands.

My mother works in social services. Her empathy for humanity is astounding to me. She is also a talented spatial thinker, organizing spaces, events, and spreadsheets with ease. It was my mother who said I should be an interior designer.

I remember not having strong feelings one way or the other about what I wanted to major in. When my mother mentioned interior design, it all clicked and felt right. Even so, I never could have predicted what being in the industry really meant.

Since graduating from Rochester Institute of Technology, I have worked for several firms that have been in the top one hundred in the country. I earned a reputation for client service and strong industry partnerships.

I have served the design community in the role of president of the International Interior Design Association's New England chapter and started initiatives that have built the next generation of leaders. Those efforts were recognized by the IIDA headquarters with an award for Chapter of the Year in 2015 and continue to support leadership and philanthropy through the region.

Personally, I won the IIDA Leadership Award and the Daily Journal of Commerce Phenom Award in addition to many project design awards over the years. I have engaged in professional associations and nonprofit boards and committees including NAIOP, CORENET, CREW, Rotary, Toastmasters, Design Museum Foundation, Center for Workplace Innovation's Think Tank, and Arthritis Foundation.

My commitment to education is lifelong. I have taught at the Boston Architectural College and helped to develop the curriculum for the Foundation program. I sat on the board of the Portland Waldorf School, shepherding a new strategic plan. I currently sit on the National Council for the School of Art and Design at Rochester Institute of Technology.

On the job, I worked for firms that failed, and I worked for firms that achieved global success. I built firms from the ground up, and I sold firms. I even worked in the dealer side of the industry in my summers off from college, specifically for a Haworth dealer. Later, I started a procurement firm—and later sold that business too.

Since those early days as an intern and librarian, I was always on a leadership track in the firms I worked for because I could design, manage, and do business development. It can be difficult to find a designer who has the potential to be a rainmaker—someone who generates leads and wins work for the firm. In 2022, I founded my own firm, Thunder Egg. At that point, I knew I could win work, design work, get paid for that work, and run a talented team of design professionals. It took years of trial and error, but I can say that I took the best of my prior firms when creating Thunder Egg, and my team agrees.

My road, however, is littered with my mistakes, as is the road of every successful design professional. I seemed to have a knack for rebounding from those mistakes in ways that turned them into career advancements rather than career killers.

Everyone wonders how I do it. As a mentor, I find myself repeating the stories and lessons I've learned over and over again. Every young designer asks the same questions and needs the same advice. After our sessions, I have seen my mentees make more money, win new work, connect with the right people, and get promoted. I have even seen them realize that professional practice was not for them—they needed to pivot into sales, brokerage, or development.

While co-ops and internships do help prepare recent design graduates for the culture of firms, these opportunities are limited. A book, however, can reach anyone, anywhere, at any time. There appears to be a need for this knowledge, and in my role as mentor, I wanted to meet this need for as many people as possible.

Passing on information is important to me. I want the graduates coming up behind me to get a chart of the potential dangers ahead rather than having to muddle through the same traps and mistakes as the rest of us. Success in a firm shouldn't include running through a gauntlet of interpersonal faux pas. The industry is small and insular. Everyone knows everyone else, so it's hard to hide embarrassing or big mistakes. It's hard to come back from the emotional and personal trauma of misjudging a situation and paying the price. We shouldn't have to risk it. And cutting through personal politics and limiting time and money spent on fixing people mistakes will leave more time and money for the important work of designing spectacular and revolutionary spaces.

The design industry is evolving. New technology to help us communicate our ideas visually is everywhere. We should also have a guide to help us navigate the people side of the industry. This is that guide.

SURVIVE TO THRIVE

This is not a book about *how* to do great architecture, interiors, or environmental branding. It's not a book about leadership. It's not going to solve all your issues or fix all the problems in your firm. But the lessons contained within will help designers in their first few years on the job read the unwritten cultural rules of the design industry. It will help you go from outsider to insider.

Think of it as a tool for reflection. A blueprint. A chart. A survival guide. A roadmap. The start of an industry awareness support group. The book contains the things I learned the hard way and is full of practical advice that I developed from mentoring and teaching some of the most talented designers in the profession. The stories and takeaways give general guidance that you can apply to your situation.

While this book is full of advice, it doesn't provide fail-safe step-by-step instructions. There's no guarantee that my strategies will work at every firm in every situation. People are people, after all, and as this book shows, even the principals at the highest levels can and will make mistakes.

The names and details of the personal stories I use as examples in this book have been changed, and sometimes stories have been combined or invented to illustrate a point and provide a representative example. The intention is not to call out any one particular person in the industry but to show the realities, both good and bad, that exist in the design industry and provide ways to navigate them successfully.

Things will not always go your way. Mistakes don't need to define you. People will focus on how you recover, how you integrate the lesson, and how you move on. As a new hire and junior designer, you come into a firm with a fresh perspective. That is valuable to your firm. We are in a creative field, after all, and staying inspired is an important part of the work we do. You bring inspiration and energy to the firm. This generates goodwill, as well, giving you more of a runway for learning. While I am sure Iris was surprised by my initial finish board, it was my recovery that mattered. I asked questions, and I didn't take it personally—and I gave her back a board that exceeded her expectations.

As you read this book, take what you find useful, and leave the rest. Don't feel like you have to do it exactly the way I did— your situation is going to be unique to you. The point is that this book will help you to understand our complex industry and navigate it with greater ease. By the end, you'll be on your way to not just surviving your first years in the design industry but thriving.

And the first step on your way to stardom starts even before you get the job.

PART 1

GETTING THE JOB OF YOUR DREAMS

Before you even fill out an application, there are several things you can do while you are still in school to prepare for the job hunt—and that will ultimately make that job hunt go much smoother. Below, I'll go over the major steps to getting the job of your dreams that will set you up for success, including:

→ How to network
→ How to interview
→ How to review your offer letter
→ How to go about your first day

CHAPTER 1

NETWORKING

WHEN I GRADUATED FROM DESIGN SCHOOL, I DIDN'T HAVE a job. The economy was in a recession, and few design firms were hiring. I knew I'd have more opportunities in a big city, so I took the leap and moved to Boston. It was the closest city to my parents, and it was home to the design firms I'd had my eye on since before graduating: ADD Inc and IA. Both had reputations as good places to start your career, and both were on *Interior Design Magazine*'s Top 100 Firms list. I don't know why, but I was always driven to work for the best. At some level, I think I knew it was the only way I was going to develop into the kind of designer I wanted to be.

I knew exactly one person who lived in Boston at the time, my college roommate's cousin. I didn't have any money. I enrolled in a master's program in architecture at the Boston Architectural College (BAC), rationalizing that additional credentials couldn't hurt. It provided a soft entrance into the city, with a job board for students and a roommate finder service where I could connect with other students to rent a place near campus. As anyone who went to the BAC will tell you, it takes something special to work full time and go to design school at night. I ended up leaving the program to focus on interiors after I landed a job at ADD Inc; however, the connections I made have lasted a lifetime.

Coming from a small town, I found that Boston was difficult to navigate—it was rumored that most of the city planning was originally done by paving cow paths. Every time I left my tiny apartment in Belmont, I would end up on the rotary in Harvard Square, even when that was not my destination. Every time. I eventually started taking the bus to the T and got lost far fewer times. Making the jump to Boston was uncomfortable. There were more questions than answers. But youth is the time to take risks. To get uncomfortable. To grow. Though it was scary, looking back, I'm so glad I did it.

I applied and interviewed with any place that was hiring, even firms not on my list. I must have handed out a hundred resumes. At best, I got informational interviews that gave me a look but weren't hiring for any open roles. At worst, I got a kind "no thank you." At least I honed my interview skills. At the time, IA was scaling back staff, and ADD was in a hiring freeze. I didn't know how it was going to happen, but after my initial interactions with their team, I had my heart set on ADD. So I went with the only thing I could: relentless enthusiasm.

I did not play hard to get.

When I got an introduction to ADD Inc's HR manager, Anne, I flat-out said that ADD Inc was the only place I wanted to work and that I would do anything to work there. In retrospect, I think this was a breath of fresh air for Anne. She was used to people playing hard ball, and here was this kid who was just desperate to work there. I met the minimum requirements: I had gone to an accredited school. I was eager. I was ambitious. I was open to learning. I knew AutoCAD and Photoshop. The rest was a function of attitude and how I would gel with the team. Anne was rooting for me. But like everyone else, ADD Inc was not hiring.

I called Anne every two weeks for two months. "Just checking in!" I would say, "Any openings?" I could hear the empathy in her voice when she gave me a soft no. Until one day *she* called *me*. She told me they had a temporary librarian position to fill, as the regular librarian was going on maternity leave. My answer was an immediate yes. Yes, I would take that temporary non-design-related position for the next twelve weeks that entailed organizing and filing the building materials product representatives brought in for designers to see and specify. Yes, I would get paid peanuts. (How did I make that work?) Yes. I knew in my soul that if I just got in the door, then it would lead to something else.

Once I was in the library, I met every material representative and designer at the firm and quickly learned the pecking order. I got in early; I left late. I organized and reorganized the materials. I learned about each one, what it was used for, and its price range and sustainability rating. I cataloged, filed, and cleaned. I loved it.

When I wasn't doing the job I was hired for, I was making myself useful to everyone I could, especially the senior designers and principals. That was when I volunteered to do everyone's finish boards and had my infamous run-in with Iris. I made myself invaluable.

The weeks slipped by, and soon it was time for my temporary contract to end. I was devastated, but they had been clear from the beginning. All the designers I had been working with over those twelve weeks went to Anne to lobby for me to stay. Team Britt was strong, but I didn't yet have the endorsement from leadership. I hadn't cultivated those relationships. Lucky for me, my fans had approached them on my behalf, and I landed a proper interview.

I turned this part-time, temporary librarian role into a full-time junior designer position in large part because I made myself useful, showed up with enthusiasm for the task at hand, and did my best.

In this example, I built a community within the firm, and I made myself indispensable. I built a network of raving fans who said that I was their secret to getting more done in less time. I didn't know it at the time, but because I was an overhead resource, my time didn't hit designers' projects, making them more profitable. These are key metrics that I would later learn are important indicators for raises and promotions. I made sure that my work was flawless, and I eagerly corrected anything that needed to be fixed. This was my first lesson in networking, which is really just building community. Do your best to help others, and together you will win.

In this chapter, I'll walk through the basics of building your network from scratch so you can land the job of your dreams.

FIRST, WHAT DO YOU WANT TO DO?

There are several specialized design staff at large firms including: architects, interior designers, and environmental branding/ graphic designers. Some firms also employ furniture specification specialists, planners, landscape architects, and engineers. Each firm has practice area specialties we call "verticals." For example, some firms specialize in hospitality only; however, other firms will have hospitality, commercial, healthcare, life sciences, and more under one roof. These diverse practice areas are the verticals within the firm.

Designers tend to specialize in larger firms both because

they may be passionate about one area of practice and because it is more efficient for the firm to keep them in one vertical. Each practice area has unique code requirements. Rather than having everyone in the firm be familiar with the nuance of every project type, like the fact that cabinets in medical office spaces need to go all the way to the ceiling so as not to create a dust shelf, it is easier and more cost effective to employ design staff that specializes in that vertical. If you are like me, you may not know what vertical you prefer out of the gate. I recommend exploring your options with job shadowing and internships at a variety of firms until you find your passion.

Once you have a vertical or a firm in mind, you can set about connecting the dots in your community. It takes all kinds of connections to build a career, and when you are starting out, it can be helpful to begin with warm connections.

WARM CONNECTIONS

Senior year of college at RIT, our professor had us make a list of firms where we wanted to apply. I had two names on my list: ADD Inc and IA. I loved the work they produced and I could see myself designing brand forward interiors for companies I admired. My professor paused on ADD Inc and said she knew a former employee who had recently moved back to Rochester. She arranged for me to meet with Chad over coffee shortly thereafter.

This was my first networking meeting, and I was so grateful that Chad would take time to meet with me. As we sat down to coffee in Fairport, New York, I pulled out my enormous portfolio to show original hand renderings, CAD floor plans, and images of my material boards. As he paged through, I held my breath, sure he would notice that my renderings were less than perfect. I was good at sketching more than rendering.

Chad flipped slowly and paused on a floor plan of my workplace project. He told me that he would make an introduction to his former colleague, Claire, and if I passed her test, she would do what she could to get me an interview. This was a step in the right direction!

I sent Claire a copy of my portfolio, a cover letter, and my resume for her to review and set up a phone interview. Claire was and is one of the sweetest, kindest people I know. We hit it off on our call, and she passed my resume along to the ADD Inc HR manager, Anne. The rest you know.

My teacher, who I'd known for years at that point, gave me my first warm connection to Chad, who warmed my connection to Claire, and then Anne, which finally led to my goal of getting hired at my dream firm. This is how it works. You build your network one connection at a time, authentically, and in the direction of your passion. Your passion is what will connect you to people and incite them to help you land your dream job.

Warm connections are pivotal to your success. A warm connection is when you know somebody who knows somebody, and they make an introduction for you. It can be as simple as, "Can you share your experience with her at this firm?" You can also make a cold connection by just picking up the phone, calling the firm's HR, and saying, "Hi. I'd like an interview, and I'm sending you my materials." That can work, too, but a firm feels less inclined to ignore someone recommended and vouched for by one of their own. When a senior designer passes your materials on to the boss, it's a silent stamp of approval, and saying no to you translates to saying no or being rude to an employee or industry contact who adds value to the firm from a cultural and profitability standpoint. It makes the job hunt so much easier, and you sound so much more valuable, when you can say, "Hello. I am following up. I believe Claire sent you my materials yesterday?" There are many ways to form warm connections, but the simple solution is to connect with as many people in the industry as possible in as many ways as possible.

Remember, everyone at the firm has been where you are now. They all applied for jobs just out of school and built strong communities to get where they are now. Most people are happy to meet with you for coffee, and after that first meeting, you are now officially linked together and ready for more warm connections in their network. Once you land a job, these early connections can help to provide a soft landing in the firm. They are uniquely qualified to help you navigate firm culture since they are familiar with the politics and have navigated the waters themselves. Having an advocate is critical to continued success within any large organization, and these early connections become your first advocates as well.

However, if you don't have a lot of industry friends to tap, there's always everyone's favorite networking tool, the cold call.

COLD CALLING

If you don't have many warm connections to work with, you can always go the route of the cold call. The trick to gaining traction with a cold call is to navigate to the right person. One tact may be to call HR and explain that you are new to the industry, having just graduated from X school, and you are looking to connect with designers to learn more about their journey, how they became successful, and if they have any advice to share. More often than not, if you have a proactive attitude, they will offer to connect you with someone on staff. They may have you come in for an informational interview. Or, they may say no. If they say no, move on to another firm.

In this day and age, email is the new cold call. A caution here, though, is that emails can get buried in inboxes relatively easily. They are also easy to ignore and easy to delete. It's harder to ignore or hang up on an actual live person.

If you do email, keep it brief. You may say something like:

Hi Anne,

My name is [your name] and I recently graduated from [your school] with a degree in [your degree]. I'm reaching out with the hope that you could connect me with someone on the design staff who I could meet with and ask questions about the industry, their path, and any advice on getting started. I am eager to learn more about the field and respect [the firm's name] work and its reputation. I know that your team is very busy, and I am grateful for any time they have to spare to help a new designer get on the right path.

Sincerely,

[your name]

[Link to your portfolio/resume if you have it]

Many of the emails I get ask if I would be open to grabbing a cup of coffee and having a chat about my experience getting started in the industry. I love these requests because I like to help people find the right fit for them, and more often than not, I am able to bring a firm they haven't heard of to their attention—one that is hiring and has an aesthetic that the person resonates with. It's rewarding for me, my coffee companion, and the firm where they get hired.

It takes guts to reach out to someone you don't know and ask them to help you. Remember, fortune favors the bold. Now that you have set up your coffee meeting with either warm or cold connections, let's go over some guidelines.

GETTING COFFEE

Before going to my coffee meeting with Chad that would start me down the road to getting hired at ADD Inc, my professor gave me some advice: be polite. Bring my portfolio and a copy of my resume, and have a list of good questions. And pay for the coffee (or at least my own). If they insist on picking up the check, however, I should graciously accept their generosity.

I dressed like I was going to an interview: black pants, white button-down shirt, and a scarf. Without the scarf, I looked too much like I was going to work at my then catering job, which made me feel a bit self-conscious—we are in design, after all, so dressing creatively is encouraged.

When meeting with new connections, there are a few talking points that are easy and helpful to work into the conversation. Ask them about the culture in their firm, their most memorable project, what they have learned working there, and how they got their start. Be genuinely interested in their story, and listen to what they have to share. Build a bond with them, and if it feels appropriate, ask for an introduction to another person in their network to continue building your community. Leave this meeting with action items to ensure that you are connecting and learning how to effectively plug into the industry. Send a thank-you note. Rinse and repeat.

Keep the tone light. This is a conversation without an agenda and less goal-oriented toward hiring than an interview. The basic expectations are to get introductions to people who value your strengths, and the person on the other side of the bistro table can assess these strengths and help make a match for you through their more developed network. It's about getting guidance on the next step toward a job you'll love with an employer who will appreciate you.

The longer you're in the design industry, the more you realize how interconnected everyone is. If there are six degrees to Kevin Bacon, there is one degree of separation to every designer inside the industry. As someone just getting out of school, you don't know those degrees of separation yet, but your coffee companion might.

Meeting in person is always better than meeting on a phone call or remotely over a video call. There is something about connecting with another person's energy in the same room that will never be replicable in a remote meeting. If possible, make every effort to meet them somewhere that is convenient for them. That way you have a better chance of connecting in person.

Coffee shops are a good place for first meetings. They're slightly informal, and the space is usually well designed and comfortable. If you choose well, they are quiet enough for a conversation. You don't have to like coffee either. Most shops offer other drinks—such as tea, water, or smoothies—ensuring everyone can find a beverage they like without too much effort. You can also meet for as long as is practical. A coffee conversation can last twenty minutes or two hours, unlike a meal or drinks, which have finite timetables associated with them.

If a connection suggests a space you are not comfortable meeting in, suggest another. "I heard the coffee here is great, and it is a one-minute walk from your office." Something like this will help you navigate choosing the right setting.

Now that you have their attention, you can ask your questions.

INFORMATIONAL INTERVIEW

One thing you can ask for during a cold call or coffee meeting is an informational interview. This sounds a little formal, but there are no stakes to this meeting since it isn't usually tied to an open position. Think of it as preliminary research on the firm to see if you even want to work there. The purpose of this kind of interview is for you to explore what the firm could offer in terms of culture and work and for a designer in the firm to expand their own network and connect with a potential prospect for the next open junior position.

If you get an informational interview via a cold call with a person at the firm you want to work for, it will most likely be someone HR has matched you up with. Someone who went to your school, lived in the same city or state, or has the same design interests. A good HR person will try to find someone compatible with you.

Here are a few questions to ask at an informational interview:

- What are the practice areas you specialize in? (This would be their verticals.)
- How long have you been with the firm?
- How many people work at the firm?
- What types of projects are you working on now?
- What are the firm's values?
- Does the firm have a mentorship program for junior designers?
- What other learning and professional development opportunities does the firm offer?
- Does the firm do any community engagement work (e.g., volunteering)?
- Does the firm support continued education? How do you monitor mentorship so that junior staff get the right types of experience?

Asking about educational opportunities in these early exploratory interviews, before you even apply, can help determine which firms go to the top of your list. Honing your craft takes commitment. In our field, technology, codes, and trends change frequently, making it important for us to continue to learn throughout our careers and especially as we enter the field. It's important to find a firm that will support your learning when you are new and as you climb the ladder.

The agendas of informational interviews are a little more formal than coffee meetings. The person across from you knows you have an idea of what you want to do and that you are interested in a job at their firm. They will expect you to ask questions related to the firm. They may invite you to tour the firm or come back for a job shadow day, which may allow you to meet more designers and discover which parts of the job you are most excited about.

JOB SHADOWING

A job shadow, at its most basic, is a day when a prospective designer comes into a firm and follows an employee around to see a behind-the-scenes day in the life of a designer at that firm. The prospective designer goes to all the meetings on the calendar that day and observes the day-to-day tasks of the designer. A well-planned shadow day offers a variety of activities, and the prospect may do a little design sketching or participate in a presentation. For example, a shadow day I planned for Thunder Egg included a tour of a lighting company's showroom, a charette design for a local nonprofit's new building, and a tour of a project under construction.

The idea is to give the shadower a small window into a typical day at the firm. For students still getting used to the industry and how things work, job shadowing helps them figure out if this industry is for them and the industry vertical on which they might like to focus. It also provides a key networking opportunity where the job stakes are low. Of course, a good impression during a shadow day could lead into a job right out of school, which is an added bonus.

Getting a job shadow opportunity is fairly straightforward: ask for one when you meet designers. School networking events like portfolio days provide opportunities for making connections like this. If you know someone in a firm or know someone who knows someone in a firm, ask them to call and request a shadow day on your behalf. Do multiple shadow days at a variety of firms, such as an architecture firm, a commercial design firm, and a development company. Be open and curious, and listen—you are sure to make a good impression.

You don't have to already have an established relationship or formal introduction to get a job shadow opportunity. I've offered job shadow opportunities to people I've just met. For instance, I was getting coffee at one of my favorite shops in Portland one Saturday. The peppy barista who helped me fawned over my coat, asking where I got it. "It's cold in Eugene, and I like to be cozy," she said, referring to a smaller city nearby, "especially when I'm going to my 8:00 a.m. class. Have you ever been to Eugene?"

"As a matter of fact," I said, "I've done many critiques at the University of Oregon in Eugene for their design department."

"Oh my god!" she gasped. "I just graduated from U of O's design program! I don't know what I want to do yet and I'm trying to figure it out!"

"Well," I responded as I handed her my card, a small smile on my face, "if you ever want to shadow me for a day, come on by."

She came to visit me a few weeks later.

Serendipitous connections happen all the time. A little positive energy, a complimented coat, and you might find the stranger across from you has a connection to the work you want to do. You never know where your next networking opportunity will come from, so be prepared to jump on it when you get a chance. And at least for the design industry, assume people want to help you. If they don't, there's no harm in approaching them, and you can move on if your overtures end with a no.

The barista's energy and willingness to open up gave me a good vibe. Complimenting my favorite coat didn't hurt. So when I found out I could help her along her career path, I did. Coincidences, fate, or good vibes floating through the universe—call it what you will, but the more effort put into connecting, the more opportunities come your way. The founder of one global firm famously got a gig designing stores for what is now a leading clothing brand by sitting on a beach next to the firm's founder and talking shop. He built the firm one project at a time to grow from a small California startup to the juggernaut it became. The barista got a job shadow opportunity with a firm founder by selling her coffee and liking her coat.

Friends new and old play a twofold role in helping land you a job. They could be connected to a firm you like, or they could help build your confidence and sense of community in the industry. In both aspects, they pave the way toward being an insider.

Most opportunities in this industry come from people who know you, whether that's leads on an open position or leads on projects and clients. So knowing a lot of people and keeping those connections warm and positive, even with something as quick and simple as a genuine compliment, makes your life easier in the long run. Senior designers with healthy networks don't even apply to jobs if they want to switch firms. They just ask those in the know who's hiring and contact the people they know in that firm. If the designer is well liked and known for doing good work, the hire is almost assured.

PROFESSIONAL ORGANIZATIONS AND INDUSTRY EVENTS

There are professional organizations for almost everything, and most of them host events, awards, continuing education opportunities, and networking opportunities for their members.

The major professional organizations in the architecture, interiors, and environmental branding world are AIA, IIDA, ASID and SEGD. There are additional organizations that relate to the industry as a whole, which we will dive into later, and even more specialized organizations like the Retail Designers of America and the National Kitchen and Bath Association that we will not cover here but can be wonderful resources as you start to specialize in those verticals. American Institute of Architects (AIA) pertains to architects. International Interior Design Association (IIDA) and American Society of Interior Designers (ASID) both serve interior designers. Historically, IIDA takes care of commercial interior designers, and ASID assists residential interior designers. Both organizations have dynamic memberships with educational opportunities in overlapping verticals. The Society of Environmental Graphic Designers (SEGD) serves graphic designers who work with the built environment. I recommend joining the student or associate levels of the professional organization that pertains to your interests and taking advantage of the educational and networking opportunities the organization offers.

As an example, I joined IIDA early in my career. I was looking for a way to connect with the design community and volunteered for the director of students role on the New England chapter's board of directors, reasoning that I was recently a student myself and could empathize with what the student members wanted.

In that role, I met some of my closest friends and colleagues, learned how to motivate teams, planned and executed events for students that connected them to jobs, and helped the chapter to increase student membership—thereby expanding the community of designers that would benefit from the initiatives led by the chapter. This early volunteer role exposed me to product reps who would become instrumental in helping me to land new jobs, win new work, and build my brand within the industry.

Listening to the students was my top priority, and what they told me they wanted was to connect with professionals who were hiring. To meet that goal, we brought back a popular event called Portfolio Day, where students would sit at long tables with their portfolios in front of them, and industry professionals would sit across the table for ten minutes in a speed dating version of interviewing. At the end of two hours, the portfolios were ranked, and the best portfolio won a fabulous prize, like a Knoll Generation Chair. It also attracted the attention of the professionals who were looking to hire talent. Winners typically walked away with great job offers. Years later, I had the honor of reviewing portfolios and hiring a Portfolio Day winner myself.

Shortly after my time as director of students, I took up the helm of president of the New England chapter of IIDA. As a leader, I have always looked to be of service rather than to come packing my own agenda. I wasn't sure that I would make a good president because I didn't have a clear vision for the future of the chapter, and I turned down the nomination twice before accepting. My longtime friend and colleague Andrea had been the one to approach me. I told her I didn't have a vision for the chapter, and she told me that was perfect. I should just listen and lead from the heart. I took the leap, and it's still one of the best things I ever did. I am so grateful to her for pushing me to stretch before I was "ready."

In that role I got to see firsthand how a leader can make lasting change in people's lives and lift up communities. The thing I wasn't expecting was how much I grew personally. Serving as president unlocked something in me that I didn't know was there. I could see the chessboard and help to align resources to give people what they needed to be successful. The year I was president, we won Chapter of the Year, an award given out annually by IIDA's headquarters. It was the cherry on top, of course, but it was what we did to earn that award that I am most proud of. It all started with Cara. I met with each board member as part of my onboarding to hear what they wanted for the chapter. Cara had been disappointed with the structure of the board and noted that only VPs got to vote. As a director, her vote didn't matter, and she felt that she was wasting her time. She left the board, and I was resolved to change the bylaws. That one change shifted the entire playing field on the board. With an equal vote, now each board member was fully recommitted to the work of making the chapter grow. The new foundation made way for categorical change in how the chapter served its members.

The second thing we did was to host a roundtable for firm leaders throughout the region. We held it in an exclusive location that most people had never been to, which built a sense of excitement, and hired a speaker everyone wanted to hear from. That got people in the door. Before they left we had just one request: write down on the card in front of them what they wanted from the chapter. Boom. The agenda was set. Based on that one two-hour program, we got twenty-four months of action items that had principal buy-in.

We implemented an Emerging Leader Program, overhauled the communications, updated the branding, started a Philanthropy Committee who donated thousands of dollars to local charities, and provided relevant continuing education credits (CEUs). The marquee events the chapter had been putting on for years were expanded and upgraded as well. We started an I Am IIDA campaign to put faces to our membership. Inspiring leaders were interviewed on video about why they were members and what the chapter had done for their career. We played these interviews at major events. Membership soared.

Personally, my volunteer days with IIDA set the stage for my personal growth and connections. I found my people. As you discover how you fit into the industry, look for your people.

INTERNSHIPS

During my time in college, including summer breaks, I immersed myself in the world of design through internships at various local firms in and around Rochester, New York, near my undergrad campus. This hands-on experience included stints at a diverse range of establishments, including a prominent local firm specializing in workplace and healthcare projects, a boutique residential designer's studio, a bustling furniture dealership, and even RIT's in-house facilities team that oversaw projects of all scales on campus.

Internships allow you to get your feet wet in a relatively low-stakes environment. You are expected to make mistakes, and your bosses expect to give you feedback to help you grow. Internships can turn into something more permanent, but usually they are steppingstones. Sometimes it's freeing to know the position is temporary, so you are more willing to explore design-adjacent roles you wouldn't normally pursue for a full-time position. This ultimately helps you to build understanding and trust on your projects later in life if you do decide to stick with design, or it might ignite a passion you didn't know you had for sales.

THE FOLLOW-UP

Regardless of how you made a connection, it's always good to keep yourself at the front of your new connection's mind by following up. Especially for one-on-one meetings, the follow-up also serves as a thank you. Let's say you learn on your coffee day that the designer meeting with you wanted a darker roast than the coffee shop served. Send over a bag of premium dark roast as a thank you and to prove you pay attention and are grateful for their time. This helps enhance a client's experience too. The follow-up and thank you shows you value the other person's time and energy.

NETWORKING BUILDS COMMUNITY

Networking is just another term for building a community. The stronger your community, the better you are able to align with the right positions, bring on the right colleagues, and ultimately craft a career that aligns with your vision for your life.

When you connect with colleagues, clients, and industry professionals, you build trust, and that trust can lead to new doors opening up for you and for them. Take every opportunity to meet new people and get curious about them, their stories, and how they fit into the industry. In the early days, especially, your inexperience can be an asset. It is a free pass to ask any question, meet any person, and get involved in as many things as possible. You can narrow your focus later. Right now is the time to absorb all you can with an open mind.

The takeaway on pre-interview networking is this: people are eager to help as long as you show an interest in starting a conversation. The design industry is small, and building goodwill goes a long way toward cementing your place in the community.

CHAPTER 2

APPLYING

KIM'S PORTFOLIO IMMEDIATELY CAUGHT MY EYE. HER PAGE layouts felt like a magazine spread, showcasing beautiful renderings layered with materials and an editorial-style description of each project in Avenir font—a favorite among designers. The software she used was clearly noted, making it easy to see her proficiency in both communication and design. Her work was elegant and thoughtful, with a strong concept that guided the design like a North Star. Beyond the craft and communication, Kim's portfolio included well-executed lighting plans and technical drawings. I saw this portfolio years ago, but I still remember it vividly.

While you finish school and start building those warm connections, you are also preparing your application materials that will be your personal brand guide in both informal and formal interviews.

Here are some must dos and some should dos as you build and share your brand and look for a job.

BUILDING YOUR PERSONAL BRAND

Your personal brand is how you are seen in the context of the industry. Whether you craft your personal brand intentionally or let it come together more organically, you definitely have one. Designers are evaluated on their portfolio, their social media presence, how they put themselves together, their attention to detail, their passion for their work, etc. In commercial design your personal aesthetic isn't as important as your ability to express your clients' aesthetic, although you may find that you are drawn to certain firms that have a specific style that mirrors your own.

In my career, I had a reputation for being a hard worker with the ability to successfully translate my clients' brand and functional needs into their space. I was efficient and able to come up with solutions that met the budget and the schedule. Because I considered how design solutions would be implemented, more of my designs got built, and I was more successful at standing out among my peers than others. An important part of my ethos has always been to have a "firm first" and "client service" mentality. It was not intentional; it was organic. However, it wasn't until I sat down to update my portfolio for the third time that I really understood this as my differentiator—what made me stand out from other applicants. Putting intention into this iteration of my portfolio, and therefore my personal brand, set me up for success in a role where I was able to learn more and help more clients.

Consider these questions:

- What are your strengths?
- What areas would you like to improve?
- What is your vision for your career?
- How do you fit into a team?
- What are you passionate about?

In addition to your unique qualities, there are a few charac-
teristics the industry values overall that will help you get ahead:

- Desire to learn and grow your skills
- Willingness to accept feedback and act on it
- Willingness to help solve pain points for others
- Being proactive and having a sense of urgency in getting things done
- Desire to contribute your interests and energy to the firm's success

It is important to set aside your ego. This can be a challenge in a creative field. Shifting your focus from "your idea" to "our ideas" can help you begin to develop the kind of mentality that will put the client and the firm first. Now this does not mean that you should let a firm walk all over you—that kind of culture is toxic, and I don't recommend working for a firm that would take advantage of you. I am talking about contributing to a greater whole and the amazing things that can come from designing as part of a team.

In the early days, you may find that your primary contribution is drafting or producing 3D renderings. Doing your job efficiently with a positive attitude and excellent attention to detail will make you a valuable team member. It will build trust with your colleagues and may eventually lead to more responsibility.

Every touchpoint you have with a potential employer will factor into how they see you aligning with the firm culture. When applying, it can be helpful to have a specific firm in mind and craft your materials to coordinate with their brand voice.

In all this tailoring to others, though, don't forget that your own personality and unique set of skills is what the firm will ultimately hire. That is the missing piece they need to balance out their team. So keep your personality present. Gesture toward the firms you love, but don't copy them. Your brand needs to look like it fits in their brand story, but yours is a unique character. When everything is said and done, emphasize who you are and what you have to bring to the table.

Let's review your application materials, your social media, and where to find firms that are hiring.

COVER LETTER, RESUME, AND PORTFOLIO

Cover letters are not as common as they were in the past. Now, candidates may send an email to a hiring manager in lieu of a formal cover letter. Your goal with this communication is to convey the following:

- Your interest in a position with the firm
- Your connection with this firm specifically
- Your value to the firm
- Your gratitude
- Your next steps

For example:

Hi [Person you spoke to],

It was a pleasure speaking with you yesterday. Working for [insert firm name] has been a dream of mine since learning about [specific project]. The impact [firm] is having on the built environment is impressive, and I would be honored to one day be part of the team bringing buildings like these into our community.

As discussed, I am graduating in June and looking for a full-time designer position. I have attached my resume here and a link to my portfolio. If you feel my skills match an opening in your firm, I would love the opportunity to come in for an interview.

If now is not the right time, I understand; however, [firm] is my top choice, and I would like to stay in contact for any future opportunities that may arise.

I'll follow up this coming Friday and look forward to next steps!

Thank you,

[Your name]

You'll want to be as specific as possible on why you resonate with this firm. Remember, you are looking to build a connection and incite action that will help you to get the job of your dreams.

Let's say that your note piques the hiring manager's interest. They will then look at your resume to evaluate it for basic skills. The skills that most hiring managers at the top firms are looking for relative to architectural and interiors candidates are as follows:

- Revit and AutoCAD
- SketchUp
- Enscape and other rendering software
- Adobe Creative Suite (Photoshop, InDesign, Illustrator)
- Microsoft Office (Word, Excel)
- Outside interests (art, nature, photography, travel, furniture making, etc.)

There are other software and skills that are specific to certain roles, but these are the major ones for junior designers and the ones that will mean getting an interview or getting a "no thank you."

Once you have checked the box on skills, a hiring manager will want to view your portfolio. I have mixed feelings about this. The goal of your cover letter and resume is to get an interview. Showing them your portfolio without the ability to explain your work could turn them off. However, it is commonplace to send a link to a portfolio website or to attach a few examples along with your resume. Follow your intuition here. If you think your portfolio stands up better when you can explain it, then send a few thumbnails with descriptions as "work samples," and tell them that you welcome the opportunity to review your full portfolio over coffee or a formal interview if appropriate.

A work sample continues to pique interest and may land you an interview. If they are hiring or are interested in learning more about you, this should set you up for success. The document should be well laid out, clear, and free from any typos and should provide them with an example of how you present yourself and your work. Typically, a work sample will have two to three examples of your school or professional work, represented by a single rendering or technical drawing. It doesn't need to be complicated; it just needs to build interest.

If you have a strong portfolio that can stand on its own, excellent. A popular way to showcase portfolio work is a website. There, you can post your resume, a bio, and your work all in one place. The graphics and layout should be flawless while also communicating your personal brand.

The content of your project work should demonstrate a range of skills (see above for the ones hiring managers are looking for) and call out what software you used to prepare the visuals so that hiring managers can see the level of your proficiency with the tools used.

Every hiring manager has their own pet peeves when reviewing a candidate's work. My personal pet peeve is when student work doesn't meet a basic level of code compliance or Americans with Disabilities Act (ADA) guidelines. Getting familiar with these necessary rules of the road and ensuring that your work complies will set you apart.

The whole portfolio should show a high level of craftsmanship and thoughtfulness in how you put things together. Images used for school should have been reformatted and standardized so everything is easy to understand, there's a text hierarchy and a logical order of information, and everything is branded cohesively and looks like it all belongs in the same body of work. The whole portfolio must tell a story.

Your ability to communicate your design is more important at this point than the actual design work itself. In the beginning you will be communicating other people's ideas and designs, and they want to ensure that you are able to do so effectively. Your portfolio is the audition for that role.

This book is not intended to be the authority on putting together perfect application materials. There are other resources that cover this in depth, and I recommend you put the effort in to get it right. What I cover here is what a hiring manager is looking for, in my experience, and the things that can set you apart.

Standing out is an important aspect to getting a competitive role. I know one graduate who got an interview because she sent her portfolio in a custom box. It sat on my boss's desk for a week, and every day my boss would say, "I have to interview this woman." And my boss did. She didn't end up getting the job—her experience and technical skills did not match the role we were hiring for at the time—but she got that first look because of her handcraft. She stood out, and that is the goal.

Design is a tactile industry. We deal in colors and textures and materials with weight and shape. Other industries may think textured, thick paper is a little over the top, but for us it's a delight. If you can find a way to play to the senses with your application materials, show you know how to put a presentation together, or send something physical as a follow-up thank you, you'll be that much more memorable.

SOCIAL MEDIA

When a hiring manager is serious about interviewing you, they will likely view your social media accounts. This shows them a bit about your personality, what is important to you, and how you present yourself to friends and family as well as a wider audience.

At this moment, LinkedIn is the primary social platform for professional designers. Many creatives also share their work on Instagram. Both platforms should showcase your professional brand with intention. If you have a social media account that you do not want a hiring manager to see, I recommend that you make it private. Many designers maintain private accounts for myriad reasons. It's okay to keep personal and professional separation here.

LinkedIn provides a platform to post your resume, portfolio link, and bio. I have made more than a few introductions by seeing who my LinkedIn connections are connected to and requesting introductions. Building your community through LinkedIn helps warm connections. You can research what potential colleagues are passionate about and find common interests.

When setting up your account, consider your photo, banner, and headline carefully. Each should communicate your brand voice clearly. If working for an informal, fun-loving firm is important to you, consider making your headshot something unique and evocative of your aesthetic. For example, when interviewing for a gaming company's headquarters, I made avatars for all our team members and listed their superpowers. It took me fifteen minutes and built a lasting rapport.

In your headline, consider adding details for what vertical you are looking for a job within. For example, "seeking a junior design position in hospitality." The specificity will help you connect with the right people.

You also have the ability to note that you are "open to work." Putting that mark on your profile helps hiring managers to understand if you are interested in openings without having to interpret your headline.

In your Work Experience section, highlight soft skills that contribute to your growth as a designer, leader, and well-rounded team member. For example, if you worked in sales at Sephora, you may be able to highlight how you managed a team, provided excellent customer service, or assisted with merchandising.

Join interest groups, as well, to follow important industry news. People will self-publish papers and thought pieces that you can interact with and learn from. These will also give you potential talking points in interviews.

FINDING JOBS

As mentioned, your network will help you find open positions to apply to, and you can always send in your materials to your top firms even if they are not hiring at the moment. There are a few other places you can look for open positions: LinkedIn, Indeed, and AIA, IIDA, and ASID online job boards. You can check individual firms' websites periodically for new postings or cold call them and ask to be notified when they have a position open (though don't rely on them to call you back). You could work with a recruiter, though it can cost money and isn't common for people fresh out of school. It is an option to consider if it's your second job.

GET IN THE ZONE

When it comes to applying for jobs, building your personal brand with intention will help you align with the right opportunities. Be meticulous as you prepare your materials. Leverage your network. Visualize a successful interview, and it is sure to line up for you.

CHAPTER 3

THE INTERVIEW

THIS IS THE FIRST TIME I'M TELLING THIS STORY, SO please, have some grace. I'm betting all of us have at least one industry story that makes us roll our eyes or reddens our cheeks when—or if—we tell it.

A huge global firm that did all the buildings for a major athletic shoe company and won international awards called me to do an informational interview. It was a big deal for me. Not only was it my first interview out of school, but the job market was in a downturn, and no one was hiring.

My mom, who lived in Seattle at the time, where the firm was located, had urged me to apply, perhaps envisioning me living close enough to come home every holiday. The firm was located in a giant skyscraper in downtown Seattle. Everything was glass and metal and stone. The soaring lobby made it feel like I'd stepped into an episode of *Succession*.

"Can you come up with me?" I asked, glancing at my mom as we stood just inside the front entrance, letting our eyes adjust to the interior lights. I'd worn a black cardigan with a robin's-egg-blue J. Crew shell underneath. Black pants and black loafers completed my look.

"Ah," my mom started, surprise washing across her face, "why don't I just wait in the building lobby?"

I'd flown in from Boston where I'd been going to school, and I didn't have a car there. The city was strange to me, so my mom had offered to drive me to the interview to make sure I wouldn't get lost and be late. Her intent was to drop me off and then wait for me at a respectable distance.

"Um, no," I insisted, glancing up again at the soaring ceilings. "I want you to come up with me."

So during my first interview ever with the number-four design company in the world, my mom sat demurely in the room behind me on the twenty-third floor, dressed in jeans and a white cotton sweater. I'm sure the woman in the power suit in front of me tried extra hard not to shoot her glances.

That I'd gotten the interview at all was practically a miracle, and the rather nice HR person who talked to me didn't let on that the questions I asked her were things I could have easily found online. By my perception, the whole interview was a disaster, and I wasn't surprised when I didn't get a call back. It only struck me years later how weird it looked to cart my mom through the office door like a living accessory. At least you'll have this pro tip about leveraging your parents when job hunting. Practice the interview with your mom, sure. Go out to debrief afterward with your mom, absolutely. But don't take her to your interviews.

Mine was a mistake just like any newbie makes starting out. I was nervous. It was a prestigious firm in the Seattle area, and I hadn't expected anything to come from my cold call. We all get nervous, especially starting out. Interviewing, taking those steps toward being an actual adult and contributor in a real firm, is a big deal. But we all take our own baby steps, make mistakes, and sometimes do embarrassing things out of ignorance or emotional needs. Forgive yourself and move to the next opportunity.

So what's a better way to do it?

To ace the interview your networking has helped you land, you'll want to follow the best practices (other than not bringing a parent) included in this chapter.

THE BIG PICTURE

Here are the key notes you want to hit in your interview:

- Demonstrate professionalism and teamwork
- Show your craft, skills, and software proficiency
- Explain how you want to grow with the company
- Recognize that you may need to build up your skills before entering the gig economy if that is a goal

To make a good impression, it is essential to demonstrate your craft, skill, and proficiency with any relevant software. Additionally, showing your personality and explaining how you want to grow with the company can help build a strong bond with the hiring team. It is also important to remember that during an interview, you are not only being evaluated on your technical skills and qualifications alone, but also on your ability to represent yourself professionally. An employer wants to know that they can trust you to represent their company in a positive light and that you will be a team player.

THE PROCESS

The hiring process can vary depending on the firm doing the hiring and the role that they are hiring for. In my experience, junior design positions at top firms typically require two interviews. However, smaller firms may only require one. As you progress in your career, you may find that there is no formal interview at all; instead, the hiring manager already knows you by reputation, and an "interview" might consist of having lunch with the hiring manager to ensure a personality fit.

In my initial interview with ADD Inc, I had already been working there for three months as a temp and had not gone through the same interview process my peers had gone through. In some ways, this helped. In others, it was harder. While I had strong relationships in place, I also felt that I had more to prove. Ultimately, my portfolio wasn't as strong as others'; however, my relationships prevailed, and my work during my temp position demonstrated my abilities, earning me a place on the team.

As you interview, keep in mind that a hiring manager is looking at your work and your personality. There are things they can teach a candidate, and there are things that they can't teach. Being eager to learn and fun to work with goes a long way, especially in the early days of your career.

PRACTICING YOUR INTERVIEW

It is normal to feel anxious during an interview or during any big presentation for that matter. Crafting a thoughtful presentation rather than showing up to an interview cold demonstrates your presentation skills, showcases your work, and guides the conversation.

For one interview, I put together a deck (professional-speak for a presentation of slides) that had three pillars: client service, residential, and workplace. The deck began with a brief bio that highlighted key points from my resume, ensuring that anyone joining the interview who had not had the benefit of seeing my resume ahead of time felt up to speed with my background enough to participate in the meeting. I then spoke about how my clients have always come first—that every design solution is inspired by the issue we need to solve and the company's brand voice and builds a community through interiors. This helped me to feature my dedication to team-based design processes as a foundational part of each design and demonstrate that I am a team player. I then dove into my project work, showing photos and design process images according to the verticals I had outlined. At the end of each section, I listed all clients I had worked with in each vertical to show the interview team that we had similar connections, building rapport and social buy-in. I wasn't nervous, even though conventional wisdom would have said that I should be: the job I was looking to leave was making me physically sick each day I was there. Because I had a logical, well-curated presentation, I knew I had given it my all.

Before showing up to this interview, I practiced. I practiced on my own. I practiced by recording myself. I practiced with one of my four roommates. I practiced with my best friend. I arranged and rearranged my slides until the flow felt right. I printed the package out in case the screen in the meeting room didn't work. I was ready. I got there early and sat in the Panera on the ground floor of the office building for forty-five minutes, and I was still early when I finally went upstairs at 8:55 a.m.

I nailed that interview, and it set me up for success within the firm, as I had demonstrated my ability to design, present, and work within a team.

If you are looking to enhance your presentation abilities, I highly recommend looking into your local chapter of Toastmasters. This organization provides a clear rubric for giving compelling speeches and offers you a platform to practice in a supportive environment where everyone is trying to improve. It's wonderful to see such a diverse group of people working on this important skill and supporting each other. I have been part of two different Toastmaster groups—one in Boston and one in Portland, Oregon. Each had members who were lawyers, healers, writers, students, designers, contractors, marketing professionals, business owners, politicians, private investigators, insurance adjusters, dragon boat racers, and so much more. It's where I learned to speak without "filler" words (like, um, ah, uh), which is critical to giving a compelling presentation.

As well as confidence in talking about yourself and your work, you'll also want to practice being gracious to your audience. No matter what happens in the interview, you want to be diplomatic and curious. In other words, practice your professional filter. You can be assertive in what you say, but not aggressive or offensive. Since you've already practiced this while networking, if you've found a tone that works, use that when you step into your interview.

HOW TO DRESS THE PART

You already know to bring your portfolio and resume. Those should never leave your side. Review your materials, and have extra copies for the interviewer to take in case they want to show other people. In addition to presenting what you can do, you also want to present who you are, and how you dress and accessorize can pull you ahead of the pack.

In a hilarious commentary on the unwritten dress code of designers, a colleague made an Architect Barbie for fun. It looked so real I thought I could buy it. Architect Barbie wore the proverbial black turtleneck, dark-wash jeans, and flat shoes. Her red hair was cut into a longish bob. A safety vest completed the look, and she was accessorized by a ruler, a tiny Moleskine notebook, and a box of Chinese takeout for those late work nights.

You'll find that many people dress in creative casual or in a uniform that they can wear to meetings, events, and interviews.

In my experience, most designers carry Moleskine notebooks and Pilot Razor Point pens. Never bring a ball point pen. Designers tend to be stationery nerds, and having the right stationery can be a point of connection with your interviewer.

While it would be odd to bring Prismacolors to your interview, I do recommend that you find an opportunity to sketch or show your hand sketches as part of your portfolio. Many hiring managers are looking for talent who can communicate their ideas via pen and paper—as that is often all we have to work with when we are in the room with a client working through an idea. So many designers rely on software to communicate their design ideas and have not developed their hand sketching abilities, so if you have these skills, be sure to demonstrate them.

The bag you carry will also send a message. Something unique and fashion forward may be appropriate and spark interest; however, reliable favorites include Kate Spade/Jack Spade, Coach, or Timbuk2, the latter if you are looking to send a more informal message.

For a recent graduate, buying expensive clothing and accessories can be a stretch, but one good ensemble and the right key pieces are an investment in your future and may be the small difference that helps build rapport with your interviewer.

Architect Barbie may be your day-to-day outfit; however, for your interview you will want to step it up a notch. Make sure that your outfit is comfortable, clean, ironed, and well put together. We are in a creative field, so a fun patterned button-down or top with black pants may be appropriate. In general, I steer toward a more conservative outfit on a first interview and then match the style of the firm once I have toured the office and seen the vibe for myself. No one is going to think less of you for dressing up, but they might think less of you for dressing down.

Over the years, I have had managing directors come to me to ask me to talk to my colleagues about their outfits. I respectfully declined. I did not feel it was my place to tell a colleague how to dress, even if it was getting in their way of being promoted or being taken to important meetings. If you're curious, here are some of the issues that came up:

- Low-cut tops: I know one designer who took a lot of pride in her appearance, meticulously putting together outfits, hair, makeup, and nails to look just so. Our managing director felt that her tops were too low cut to be appropriate for the office, and he couldn't take her to meetings with our more conservative clients. If your goal is to advance in the design industry, factor in how your wardrobe may be impacting your opportunities.
- Shabby clothing: As with the low-cut tops, showing up to work in an outfit that is unkempt will likely inhibit you from advancing, attending important meetings, and representing the firm in a meaningful way.
- High heels: Heels that are too high for you to walk comfortably in can inhibit your ability to tour project sites and may limit your ability to participate in important project work.
- Sheer clothing: I have seen HR send people home for wearing sheer (see-through) clothing. Sheer clothing policies are often noted in the employee handbook under Dress Code.

While personality is good, especially nods to your creativity, I'd hesitate to go to any extremes while you are getting to know the firm culture. If what you wear is more important to you than where you work, that is okay. Just make an informed choice to maximize your options. When I interviewed for a design director position at a global firm, I did my hair in a tidy updo and wore simple makeup, a black-and-white silk top in a geometric pattern, and a pencil skirt in their signature red. Like your other touchpoints, your outfit is an opportunity to showcase to your interviewer how you fit into the firm culture. Details matter.

Even now, when presenting to a client, I coordinate my outfit to the client's brand and the design we are presenting to them. If I'm showing multiple palettes, I will coordinate to the palette I prefer. At one point I was working with three different apparel brands. In those days I often needed to go from one brand to another in one day, so I kept my outfits neutral and put a pair of hot-pink Adidas Originals, a pair of On running shoes, and a pair of Dr. Martens boots in my trunk at all times. Being ready to represent a brand in their brand voice is part of our job as designers crafting space for some of the most forward-thinking brands of our time. Your ability to step into their (literal) shoes will show an interviewer or a client that you get the assignment.

INTERVIEW QUESTIONS

By the time you earn an interview, you have likely researched the firm and discovered what types of projects they are best known for. Before you head into an interview, I recommend that you familiarize yourself with the principals and staff at the firm by searching them on LinkedIn. Here you can find overlapping connections, schools, professional organizations, and philanthropic causes that will give you talking points during your interview. Finding common ground is an essential part of creating a good rapport with the hiring team.

Preparing questions for specific individuals is ideal; however, it is not always possible to know who will be conducting your interview. Do your best to research likely interviewers, and come prepared with a few talking points that demonstrate how you align with the firm's values. For example, if you participated in CANstruction, a popular industry event that is in many cities across the US, and the firm also had an entry, you can discuss the event, what you built, and how it benefited the local food bank.

Here are a few more suggested talking points as you prepare.

COMMON ASSOCIATIONS

Is your interviewer a member of a professional organization that you are interested in? You can ask them how they have liked their membership and what events they enjoy participating in. If they are on the board, it's likely they will be happy to talk about their contribution and ways you can get involved too. Bonus: this creates a reason to follow up as well.

INSPIRING PROJECTS

Now that you have found some common ground, let them know why you want to work at their firm. Review the firm's body of work, and choose a few projects that you find interesting or that you connect with. Be specific. When I was interviewing at ADD, I was familiar with their work at the Maine Mall where they completed a refresh to the corridors and food court. I mentioned that I liked the terrazzo floor pattern I'd seen during my family's trips to the mall (which were annual, since we lived in a rural part of the state and didn't make it to "town" much). It was a point of connection that showed I was paying attention and a part of the firm's impact.

VALUES

It is important to align on values. Every firm has its pros and cons. Decide what is important to you, and work to find a firm that aligns with your values. For example, diversity can be a difficult thing to achieve in a field that has traditionally been dominated by white men. If diversity is important to you, there are firms that do excellent work to ensure diversity, equity, and inclusion initiatives are a part of their culture. Ask your interviewer to describe the firm values and culture. This should give you a good idea of what it would be like to work there, providing context for whether your values align with the firm's values.

MENTORING PROGRAMS

Whether you are just starting out or you have ten years of experience under your belt, participating in a formal mentorship program is an important part of developing as a designer. If the firm has a mentorship program, it can be a good sign that it will be an excellent place to grow and learn. Be sure to ask your interviewer how the firm supports junior designers to grow professionally.

COMPENSATION

While most talk of benefits will come later, compensation is likely to come up during your interview. If you can, let the firm tip their hand first on this one. If they ask you, "What are your salary requirements?" say, "Thank you for the question. I want to make sure that I'm valued in this position, and it is important to me that the salary offer reflects my value, so I would like you to put out the first number. Then I'm happy to respond to it." It's good to let them put out that first number, either in the interview or later in the offer letter, because the firm will almost always offer *more* money than you would have asked for. And if you ask for less than they are prepared to offer you, it may influence your starting position and your future compensation. And if *they* offer you way less than you know you're worth, then that's a sign this firm may not value your work. If they demand a number, be ready with one based on your research. As of this writing, popular sites that list up-to-date compensation statistics include the AIA Salary Calculator, Indeed, and Salary.com.

LOCATION

Where you will be working is a necessary post-COVID-19 question. Because we're in the business of making spaces, most firms still value a brick-and-mortar office and want their team, especially their junior staff, to come into that space for project efficiency, learning, and mentoring. That being said, some firms are fully remote, so you'd be working from home or potentially a coworking space in your city. While avoiding a commute can be attractive, when you are just starting out, I recommend that you look for a firm that is in-person at least two to three days per week, if not five days per week. The learning opportunities you will gain from working in person with your team are invaluable.

THE FOLLOW-UP

After your interview, you have a twenty-four-hour window to send a follow-up thank-you email to your interviewer. This is an important step and not to be missed. Candidates who do not follow up run the risk of having their interviewer assume they are not really interested in the position or that they have poor business etiquette and may not be a good fit with the firm.

If you would like to send a handwritten thank you, that is okay, but I recommend hand delivering it to reception rather than putting it in the mail so that your interviewer receives it in a timely manner.

If you don't hear anything from the firm within two weeks after your initial follow-up, then reach out—politely, of course—to check on your application. Design firms get busy, and you don't want to fall into the forgotten depths of someone's email. Renew that communication thread, and put yourself back to the top of their inbox. You can even say something like, "Floating this to the top of your inbox. Please let me know if there is any news on this position, as I am very interested in working with [the firm]." You can also make a request for further contact. "Please let me know if there's anybody else at the firm you'd like me to connect with." It's always good to keep that network growing and warm. Keep checking in every two weeks or so until you hear a yes or no.

If you still don't hear back after checking in four or five times, it's time to move on. Hopefully, you've already been pursuing other options while you wait. You don't want to work for a firm that ghosts you for that long anyway. This, of course, pertains to formal interviews. If you are following up after informational interviews, you can keep in touch until they open a position and invite you to apply or tell you that they will reach out when things open back up. Again, if you aren't on the firm's radar when a position does open, you might lose out to someone who is.

READY TO START

The best hires I have worked with were enthusiastic candidates who were eager to help in any way they could, were excited to learn, and checked their ego at the door. With a positive attitude and a bit of luck, you will be stepping into your first day in no time.

CHAPTER 4

STARTING STRONG

SO NOW YOU'RE THE TOP CANDIDATE, AND THE FIRM GIVES you an offer you can't refuse. Or can you?

I was shocked when one of my ADD Inc mentors told me that in her long tenure with the firm, only one woman on staff had ever negotiated her salary. Every other woman had taken the first offer. To drive her point home, she noted that most of the men had negotiated theirs. It was an odd thing to disclose to a junior team member, but I think she wanted me and the other junior designers to do a better job advocating for ourselves. I got a 17 percent raise that year.

Once the interview is done and the firm decides it wants to hire you, there are a few points to negotiate before accepting the position. Many people rush this stage of the hiring process, but negotiating good terms shows your hiring manager that you can advocate for yourself and will eventually be a good advocate for the firm.

There is always room for a little negotiation, even at the very beginning. So before you excitedly sign on the dotted line, take a pause, get in the headspace of a leader who reads the fine print, and negotiate your offer letter.

NEGOTIATING YOUR OPENING OFFER

A firm will likely call you to formally offer you the job and discuss the terms. They will follow up by emailing you a written offer letter. It is important to not commit to the position without first reading and understanding the offer. Once you sign it, the time for negotiation is over.

It is exciting to get an offer. However, the terms of an initial offer are usually far from the best deal you can negotiate for yourself. If you don't understand the terms, you can hire a lawyer for a basic interpretation online or seek out a business-savvy friend to help you with the fine print.

Once you understand the terms, it's time to negotiate.

THE PROCESS

The basic terms of the offer should state the salary, benefits, pay schedule, and start date. Benefits vary widely and can be negotiated in order to add value to your overall compensation package without increasing your base salary.

Typical benefits include overtime, vacation time, paid time off (sick time), retirement contributions, continuing education contributions, professional organization fees, licensing fees, work-from-home office furniture stipend, and more.

Some of these items are negotiable, and some of them are not. I recommend beginning with reviewing your base salary, which is negotiable, and building out your counter-proposal from there.

SALARY

As mentioned before, you can find up to date compensation statistics on AIA's website, Indeed, or Salary.com. For reference, my first full-time job in 2003 paid me $38,000 a year. Twenty years later, junior design staff earn upward of $55,000 a year plus bonuses. Be sure to review your compensation package annually or whenever you take on new responsibilities beyond your original job description to ensure you are being fairly compensated.

Let's say a firm offers you the median salary for designers in your position according to these sites or their own research. If they do not offer overtime pay and you consistently work overtime, you could negotiate a higher base salary by requesting a percentage increase based on your historical overtime hours. Although overtime may be part of your bonus structure, bonuses are not guaranteed, and they are taxed higher than wages. Requesting a higher base rather than a bonus will put more money in your pocket.

If a firm responds that they have salary caps for certain positions, request to see the ranges for your position and the position immediately above yours. This will help you understand the salary range and discuss the success metrics required to qualify for the higher end of the range.

In my experience, a hiring manager is often authorized to negotiate up to a 10 percent increase over the initial offer or more. Aim to ask for just enough to have the hiring manager seek approval from senior management for your salary request, as this is likely the highest limit they are willing to offer.

Securing the highest salary possible is crucial because it will serve as the basis for future salary increases throughout your career at that firm. During your annual review, your performance-based or cost-of-living raise will be a percentage of the salary you negotiate now.

BONUS

A starting bonus is a common benefit, whether you are a junior designer or a seasoned design leader. This can be particularly helpful if you have new expenses related to accepting the job, such as higher transportation costs or a benefit that your new firm doesn't provide that your prior firm did, like a gym membership. If you need to relocate for the position, you might also negotiate a bonus to help cover related costs.

Bonuses give you a quick cash infusion and celebrate your new job. However, ensure you understand any conditions attached. Many firms require you to pay back larger bonuses if you leave within a specified time frame. This can feel like golden handcuffs if things don't work out and you've already spent the money.

Annual bonuses are different and should be factored into your annual compensation package. Many firms hold aside a certain percentage of your salary as a bonus target. Find out if your firm does this and what percentage they use. It can also be helpful to ask what the performance metrics are to achieve a higher bonus than the standard allowance.

RETIREMENT

Retirement may feel a long way off, but saving as much as you can now will pay off in the future. Choose a firm that provides a retirement savings account, such as a 401(k) or IRA, which allows you to save pre-tax dollars for retirement. Your firm may also offer a matching contribution. Find out what this is, and plan to maximize it.

A unique benefit that ADD Inc provided was thirty-minute appointments with a local financial planner. Each year, I met with the planner to review my investments and strategize for the future. I was able to continue using the same planner even after changing firms years later.

OVERTIME

A reality of our industry is that most people work overtime. That may not always be the case, but if you do anticipate that you will work overtime, you should expect to be compensated for that work either hourly or by a bonus that reflects your additional effort at the end of the year. Clarify the firm's overtime policy with your hiring manager so you can factor it into your overall compensation.

TIME OFF

If a firm offers you the standard two weeks of vacation time, you can often negotiate for an additional week. If they base vacation days on title and longevity, ask to see the ranges so you know what to expect. Additionally, understand whether your vacation time is preloaded or accrued over hours worked. You might find that you haven't worked long enough to accrue enough vacation hours for that week in Mexico, leading to unpaid time off. Some firms allow immediate access to vacation time when you start. Clarify the policy to avoid any surprises later.

Paid sick leave is different from vacation time. This pool of days is reserved for when you or a family member are ill and is typically not negotiable, as it is regulated by the state. Ensure you understand the distinctions and the specific policies your firm has in place for both types of leave.

CONTINUING EDUCATION

Continuing education is a requirement of the design field. As such, many firms will reimburse you for continuing education expenses, including study manuals, testing fees, courses, conferences, trade shows, and more. Negotiate an annual stipend toward continuing education units, and if you have a few years of experience under your belt already, you may be able to negotiate an allowance toward specific trade shows or conferences. Check your firm's company handbook for the specific benefits your firm offers.

Early on in my career, I paid my way to NeoCon, a large annual commercial interiors trade show in Chicago. I stayed with a friend and got the lowest-cost airfare I could find. It didn't occur to me that my firm would be the one to determine whether I went or not—I thought of it as critical to being effective at my job and made it happen. I realized that this was not typical when people asked me, "Who is sponsoring you?" When I said, "No one," I was met with surprise. Make sure you have access to the learning opportunities that you value as you grow in your career.

PAY SCHEDULE

Pay schedules aren't usually negotiable, but you do want to know when you'll get paid so you can budget. Once or twice a month is common. You can also ask if bonuses are offered, how much they are on average for your level, and when they get distributed, usually once or twice a year.

If your firm pays staff once per month, you can ask that they run a special payroll for you in the first month to help you get on that schedule. This is fairly common if someone is coming from a firm that pays its staff biweekly.

Once you have negotiated a good deal for yourself and you sign your final offer letter, you've got the job. Go ahead and celebrate. You earned it!

So what happens after you land the job? Your first few days will be filled with onboarding tasks, meeting new people, and learning new procedures.

INTEGRATING INTO YOUR NEW DESIGN FIRM

On my first day at a new firm, the receptionist demonstrated how to make the coffee in the break room. It looked like some foreign ritual: take out the old filter, put in a new one, fill the water chamber just so, grind the beans (who does that?), measure the ground coffee precisely with a little spoon, touch all these buttons, and voila! Coffee for everyone.

"If you finish off the pot, you're responsible for making a new one," she explained solemnly, as if she was going over the safety instructions on a construction site.

I hadn't realized that the caffeine situation at this firm was so...serious.

I make terrible coffee. It always tastes like slightly bitter water or burned bark. I vowed I'd never be the one to empty the pot so my new coworkers would not have to suffer through my attempts.

As you step into your first day, you will want to pay attention to the written and unwritten rules of the firm and its culture. It's a little like the first day in a new school. In addition to learning where the copy room is, you are getting to know a whole new group of people. Pay attention to office etiquette, and be on the lookout for friends and mentors. And remember that if you're going to drink the last cup, refill the coffee.

PROCESSES AND PROCEDURES

As part of your onboarding process, you can expect to receive an employee handbook. This will contain essential legal items such as the paid time off policy and the family leave policy. Many firms will also include discretionary items like moonlighting, nondisclosure agreements (NDAs), and continuing education policies.

Moonlighting involves taking on design projects outside your full-time job at a firm. As a junior designer (and often as a senior designer), moonlighting is common and can provide extra income, which is valuable early in your career when your salary is lower than that of your more senior colleagues. However, moonlighting can expose you and your company to costly liabilities, and some firms outright ban it. Make sure you understand your firm's stance on moonlighting before accepting any side gigs.

Another common startup document is an NDA. You might want to announce that you are designing the office of the future for Google, but many high-profile clients (especially those with shareholders) require firms and their employees to agree to NDAs that limit their ability to discuss the project. The work we do on high-profile projects can impact things like shareholder evaluations and employee perceptions of company spending.

GET TO KNOW THE TEAM

Now that you are familiar with the written rules, it's time to understand the unwritten ones by building a community within the firm. On your first day, HR might set up a lunch meeting to help you get to know your new colleagues. This is your opportunity to ask good questions and learn about the firm, its culture, and its people. Ask how your new colleagues started with the firm, what projects they are working on, and what the firm does in terms of community engagement. This might include company-sponsored trips or volunteer days supporting causes aligned with the firm's values. Engaging with these opportunities will be crucial to your success in building community at the firm, so seek out key cultural points and participate.

For example, every year one of my first firms would go to a different resort in New England, such as Sugarloaf or Sunday River. The ski trip took time to plan, with discounts for staff and a celebratory dinner with a small awards ceremony after the meal. Planning the ski trip gave me the chance to connect with people I otherwise didn't cross paths with, such as the firm's principals and folks on other teams. A lot of memories were made on those trips while everybody was having fun, their guard was down, and the wine was flowing.

If your firm doesn't have company trips or other sponsored team-building activities, consider other ways to get to know your new colleagues on a personal level. Many firms set up informal meetings with firm leaders so they can get to know the next generation of talent. Use these meetings to learn about leadership's vision for the firm and to demonstrate your passion for specific areas of the business. Ask about the philanthropic organizations your firm leaders are involved in; you can learn a lot about someone by how they donate their time and money.

Building relationships across the firm will help you align with the right learning opportunities and projects. More importantly, it will build cohesion and make you feel part of something larger than yourself.

Building cohesion in the workplace also involves adhering to office etiquette. While the employee handbook might specify that flip-flops are not allowed, it often doesn't clarify what is considered appropriate attire.

While wearing flip-flops might not be considered professional in any firm, what defines the firm's professional vibe may be harder to discern. When starting work at one firm, I wore high heels, skirts with blouses, and a suit jacket to the office. On my second day, a project manager pulled me aside and said, "We don't dress so fancy here." Her intentions were good, and I appreciated the feedback, although I continued to wear my dresses and heels. Dressing this way was an integral part of my identity, and I believed that you could never be overdressed. Be intentional with the message you send with your wardrobe choices, and be mindful of the guidelines of office etiquette.

Similarly, you will want to understand the official and unofficial working hours. The official business hours may be eight to five, but is that what people actually adhere to? At one particular firm, my team was working on a deadline for a software company. I couldn't help with the remaining tasks, so at 7:00 p.m., I packed up and checked in with the team one more time before going home. The next day, my managing principal pulled me into a conference room and harshly criticized me for leaving. The time you choose to leave the office may reflect your commitment to the firm.

BE ON THE LOOKOUT FOR MENTORS

I attribute my success to a small handful of mentors who guided me through those early years. Their advice was invaluable as I navigated my career, eventually striking out on my own, selling companies, and mentoring my team. Additionally, I've had the pleasure of learning a great deal from those I've mentored over the years.

While getting the job is a significant achievement, keeping it requires sustained effort. Top firms have layers of politics, processes, procedures, and personalities. To navigate them successfully, you will need to acclimate and find a mentor. Remember how crucial it was to join a firm with a mentorship program? This is why. A good mentor will shorten your learning curve as you integrate into the firm and guide you through those critical first days.

NEGOTIATING FOR SUCCESS

As you become familiar with the written and unwritten rules, you'll start to understand the positions and personalities of your new colleagues. Your ability to integrate into the culture and connect with your peers will significantly impact your success at the firm and your growth over time.

Building these relationships and understanding the office dynamics are crucial steps in establishing yourself and thriving in your new role. Embrace the learning process. Seek out mentors, and actively participate in your firm's culture. These efforts will pay off, helping you to achieve your professional goals and contribute meaningfully to your new workplace.

KNOW YOUR PEOPLE

Now that you're an industry insider, you have to know who the players are in order to thrive. In the following chapters, you'll learn:

→ Who the players are in your firm
→ Who the players are in the industry
→ How these professionals connect to each other and the clients we serve

CHAPTER 5

COLLEAGUES

TIME SEEMED TO STOP AS GRACE OPENED HER MOUTH TO yell at me. The expression on her face is permanently etched into my mind.

She approached my librarian desk with hopeful, even happy eyes. But when she asked me about the task she had assigned, she discovered the project paperwork buried under a fresh set of carpet sample books. As I unearthed it, she screamed, "My work comes first! This work is important, and your lack of concern is, frankly, alarming. If you are not interested in helping with this task, then I will give it to someone who is. I deserve better!"

I was shocked. I had inadvertently made her feel like I didn't care about her project. The truth was, I cared very much and was grateful to be doing project work. The carpet books had been placed over her project file while I was away from my desk for a moment.

There was no saving the situation, so I profusely apologized, hoping to regain her favor. Grace had a reputation for being easily enraged. People were afraid of her, but I wasn't. Maybe it was the Mainer in me—in the summers during college, I served coffee and made pizzas for the fishermen at the general store in my hometown. They showed their affection by giving me a hard time, so I was used to winning over tough characters.

Grace was a senior associate. She had something to prove—she wanted to become a principal at the firm, and to do that, she needed to hit certain benchmarks for profitability, bring in new work, and lead her teams well. So she was tough. I looked up to her for that and didn't take offense to her lecture. If I had seen what she saw and made the same assumptions, I would have been disappointed too. I might not have expressed it the same way, but I would have been disappointed. Instead of getting upset and dismissing her legitimate concerns along with her anger, I took her reaction as feedback on how I could improve.

Understanding where people are coming from often begins with seeing through the emotion. Pause and ask how they fit into the firm. What pressures are they under? What expectations must they meet? What motivates them? This approach can build empathy as you navigate relationships and complex politics and will help you thrive in the intricate web of personalities that make up the design industry.

There are many types of firms out there, each with its own unique structure and culture. I have worked at all sizes of firms—from sole proprietorships to the largest firms in the world and everything in between. Among them, there are a few key players you'll meet consistently. If you can learn the players, their motivations, and how to navigate firm politics early, you can raise your social capital from the start and ascend the ladder faster.

It's up to you to discover how your colleagues operate and your role within the whole. You may know the basics of who's who from your interview and onboarding, but now it's time to get granular with your networking and intentionally put work into your new relationships. These relationships will help you become a more empathetic and effective teammate.

Everyone has a boss, and they are under pressure from that boss to get it right. Knowing the chain of accountability can help you understand other people's perspectives, which gives you empathy for where they are coming from and foresight into how you can help the team next.

NAVIGATING ROLES, JOB TITLES, AND HIERARCHIES IN DESIGN FIRMS

In the world of design firms, job titles can be both functional and hierarchical. A functional job title, such as architect, interior designer, or graphic designer, tells you about the daily activities of the person. A hierarchical job title, such as director of design, principal, or managing director, provides insight into their responsibilities within firm operations.

In my experience, the best projects come from integrated teams where the architects, interior designers, and environmental graphic designers all have an equal hand in how the project is shaped. For example, I was part of a team that created a headquarters for a major tech company. The company sought to create a one-of-a-kind workplace that expressed their brand identity through the space. The design team came up with graphics that spoke to the global presence and impact of the company, featuring office locations from around the world and imagery that connected people to the area of the world—including food, landmarks, and more. This integrated team was able to create a design that was exceptional and inspiring to the employees who later worked there. Below are some of the typical characters you will find on your project teams who all contribute to successful projects.

ARCHITECTS

In my experience, architects focus on designing and documenting the core and shell of a building. This includes the exterior envelope and building systems such as elevators and stair locations. An architect often serves as the code review point person on a team. For projects that are heavily reliant on environmental branding, a graphic designer may also contribute to the design of the exterior envelope. In some firms, architects take on interior design roles as well, especially if there are no dedicated interior designers. Architects typically lead construction administration, particularly when the design includes work on the exterior envelope or building systems.

INTERIOR DESIGNERS

Interior designers are responsible for the design and documentation of the inside of the building, from space planning to lighting to power and signal plans to finish selections. They frequently oversee construction administration, taking a project from inception to completion, especially if it is primarily interiors-focused, like a tenant fit-out project.

ENVIRONMENTAL GRAPHIC DESIGNERS

Environmental graphic designers weave stories through the spaces designed by architects and interior designers and sometimes have standalone projects where the entire renovation is branding- and graphics-focused. Their work emotionally connects people to the place through compelling graphics, media, and branding. Some firms involve graphic designers after the main design work is complete, while others integrate them from the beginning to craft a thoughtful experience that informs the architecture of the space.

OPERATIONS: MATERIALS LIBRARY, ACCOUNTING, MARKETING, IT, LEGAL, HUMAN RESOURCES, BUSINESS DEVELOPMENT

Larger firms typically have departments for operational functions such as materials library management, accounting, marketing, IT, legal, human resources, and business development. These roles are essential but are considered overhead rather than design staff. They ensure that resources are available, payments are processed, computers run smoothly, staffing is adequate, and the project pipeline is full. In smaller firms, these roles may be distributed among design staff leaders until the firm grows enough to require dedicated personnel.

PRINCIPAL

The title of principal is reserved for those with equity stakes in the firm. While some senior new hires might negotiate for this title, it is generally earned through demonstrating commitment and value to the firm over time. I recall a colleague who was an exceptional architect and artist. A principal at our firm admired his work both at the office and in the painting studio and felt a strong connection with him. This principal took this architect under his wing and carved out a special director role for him to grow within the company. While being a great leader and designer were key to getting this promotion, his connection with leadership helped him to expedite the path to being titled staff.

ASSOCIATE

There are multiple layers to the associate title, such as associate and senior associate. This title serves as a stepping stone to becoming a principal and often involves additional responsibilities like organizing committees or coordinating staffing.

DESIGN STAFF

This category includes all staff involved in producing designs, from 3D renderers to environmental graphic designers. These positions might be listed on business cards as junior designer or designer.

INTERN

Interns are typically temporary hires working during school breaks or as part of a co-op program. Some interns transition to full-time positions after graduation. Some firms have dynamic and engaging internship programs where staff actively mentors interns, assigning them project work, competitions, and important programming and research tasks. Other internships may be more like job shadowing. Be aware that some internships are unpaid—a practice that goes back generations. However, this is not supported among reputable firms today, and many actively lobby for firms to pay interns.

FIRM ROLE JARGON

Understanding industry jargon is crucial. Here are a few key terms:

- Architect of Record: This is the architect who stamps the drawings to certify them for permit submission. While the contractor might handle the actual filing, the architect of record ensures the drawings meet local requirements. A design architect might engage an architect of record if they aren't licensed in the area or need specialized knowledge. For instance, a design firm may hire an architect of record when working with cross-laminated timber for the first time, or a New York-based design architect might collaborate with an architect of record in Scottsdale, Arizona, if it's impractical to get licensed in Arizona for a Scottsdale project.

- Decorator: Decorators may or may not have a design degree from an accredited interior design program. They specialize in finishes and furnishings and typically do not advise on moving walls or the architectural elements of an interior. They often collaborate with other professionals on complex projects.

- Design Architect: This term refers to the firm responsible for the look and feel of a building. A design architect may also be the architect of record, but in that case, they are usually just referred to as the architect.

- Rainmaker: A person who generates significant value for the firm by bringing in projects that increase revenue.

- SME (Subject Matter Expert): Someone who is an expert in a particular area, such as workplace design or healthcare design. Within a vertical like workplace design, there can be SMEs for technology companies, law firms, or footwear. These experts provide deep insights and ensure that projects meet the specific needs of their niche.

- Specialist: A person who specializes in one aspect of project delivery, such as a detail expert, lighting designer, or rendering expert. Their expertise ensures that specific elements of a project are executed flawlessly.

- Star: A versatile individual who excels in design, business development, and team management. This person is likely to start their own firm or assume a leadership role in an existing one.

- Titled: A designation indicating that you have achieved the associate or principal level at the firm.
- Untitled: A term for design staff who have not yet reached the associate or principal level.

These terms and roles shape the structure and culture of design firms. Understanding them will help you navigate your career, build meaningful relationships, and contribute effectively to your firm. By integrating your skills with a clear understanding of these roles, you can find your place and make a lasting impact in the design world.

JOIN IN TO STAND OUT

It's hard to know where you fit in until you know all the players, so be open, be curious, work hard, add value where you can, and reserve judgment. Attend events. There will be so many events hosted by the firm, rep groups, contractors, and industry organizations. Attend everything. Meet as many people as you can. You never know who you will connect with long term, but in the meantime, you will be building your community.

A firm is an ecosystem, and everyone is working toward a goal. For me, that goal was excellence. I never liked politics, which is why I now run a no-ego firm. Some people are excellent at playing politics, and they thrive in this environment. You'll learn what kind of firm culture you like, but no matter where you go, follow the North Star of your own values, and make your own opportunities by advocating for yourself.

This last point is also good advice for navigating the wider world of the AEC (architecture engineering construction) industry and the players who populate it, which is where we're headed next.

CHAPTER 6

INDUSTRY ALLIES

NOW THAT YOU UNDERSTAND THE NUANCES OF YOUR OWN firm, it's time to look beyond the walls of your office and explore the broader network of people who shape our industry. Who are the teams that bring a project to life? Who are the people who eventually move into the spaces we design? Who designs and manufactures the furniture they use?

In this chapter, we will delve into the commercial real estate ecosystem, examining the key players and processes that drive our industry. Understanding this network will not only enhance your perspective but also empower you to navigate your career with greater insight and effectiveness.

For example, as a junior designer, one of my first tasks was to punch list a new luxury condo building in the South End of Boston. I was on-site every day, going unit by unit to evaluate the quality of the construction by scrutinizing the walls, casework, lighting, and hardware for any imperfections. I documented my findings and reported them back to the general contractor.

I quickly learned that if the union subcontractors liked you, they would mark your hard hat with a sticker representing their union. Most designers don't get these stickers, and you can identify an architect or designer by their clean, white hard hat with either their company logo or the general contractor's logo. I was proud to be accepted by the surly subcontractor crew on my project site and felt a camaraderie with them.

After that project was complete, I moved to a non-union project in the suburbs for a robot vacuum company. Unaware of the difference between union and non-union projects, I showed up with my sticker-covered hard hat, ready to walk the job site with the general contractor and client. The general contractor handed me a new, plain hard hat. "You'll, uh, want to wear this one," he said.

"No, I'm okay. I like my hard hat," I replied, shocked that he seemed unimpressed by my sticker collection (and therefore my perceived coolness).

"No, take this one," he insisted. After some back-and-forth, I reluctantly switched to the plain hard hat.

Years later, I realized my stickered hard hat, full of union insignia, would have sent the wrong message to the non-union subcontractors, who frequently had to deal with inflatable rats and protesters at their job sites. That was my first faux pas on the job, but it wasn't my last by a long shot.

Here's a breakdown of the people and their roles in the industry. Hopefully knowing who's who will help you avoid mistakes like wearing the wrong hard hat to a job site.

CLIENT

We wouldn't have projects without clients. Anyone who hires a designer for their services is a client. A client can be a developer, property manager, or end user. There can also be layers of clients with different success metrics. For example, if a multinational tech company hires your firm to design a state-of-the-art facility, it is typically the director of real estate or the VP of facilities management who acts as your "client." They often sit in the company headquarters and represent the end users—the people who will occupy the space once it is complete. The end user may sit anywhere else in the world, since IBM (and other multinational companies) has offices across the globe. The end user is also your client. The end user is also the VP of facilities management's client. Your goal, and your VP's goal, is to create a space that meets the end users' needs, conforms to any established design standards, stays within budget, and is delivered on time.

However, many clients don't have full-time facilities departments to run their projects. In such cases, your client might be the end user themselves or a combination of the end user and their representative, known as a tenant rep.

TENANT REPRESENTATIVE

A tenant representative is an advocate hired by the client to guide them through the design and construction process. Familiar with the full leasing, design, and delivery process, a tenant rep assembles the design team, general contractor, and furniture procurement specialists. They work with the client to develop the budget and advise the client on which space to lease, often working in tandem with a broker or acting as both broker and tenant rep. A good tenant rep ensures the project stays on schedule and within budget, successfully managing the team to meet design and construction milestones. Many tenant reps work for real estate brokerage companies that also employ brokers, property managers, and workplace strategists.

When you have a good rapport with a tenant rep you may find that you are invited to interview for more of their projects.

I enjoyed working with one tenant rep for three projects in a row. We found a team rhythm, and our clients appreciated the fun and efficiencies that came with that kind of history. When you find a successful partnership, keep the relationship going long beyond the last punch list.

BROKER

A broker helps clients find spaces to lease for their business. In the commercial real estate world, brokers can also assist companies in finding land for "build to suit" projects, where the landowner constructs a building specifically for the tenant. Brokers earn commissions based on the lease value and are often asked to recommend the design team.

Since brokers are often the first to know when a client is looking for space, they are our best source of new projects. Connecting with brokers can help you build your pipeline of work. I recall one sunny Thursday afternoon when a few broker friends invited me to join them on a cruise around Boston Harbor. The sky was clear, and the water sparkled. The city skyline provided a stunning backdrop as we set off. As we laid out on the bow, enjoying the sun and casual conversation, a few adventurous souls decided to jump into the harbor.

The idea of diving into the murky harbor water wasn't exactly appealing. But what's an ear infection among friends? I hesitated for a moment, weighing the pros and cons. Then I realized that this was more than just a swim—it was a chance to bond with my peers in a memorable way.

So I took a deep breath, mustered up some courage, and jumped in. The water was surprisingly refreshing, and any initial reservations quickly melted away. We laughed, splashed, and shared stories as we swam. The shared experience broke down barriers and created a sense of camaraderie that wouldn't have been possible otherwise. By the time we climbed back onto the boat, I felt a genuine connection with these new friends.

That day turned out to be more than just a fun outing. The relationships I built felt real and meaningful. We were all in the early stages of our careers, trying to navigate the industry and support each other along the way. One of these connections even led to a project with a major brand, but what I valued most was the sense of community we created. It's a reminder that the best connections often come from simply being open and sharing experiences with others. Taking the plunge—literally—was one of the best ways to truly connect.

PROPERTY MANAGER

Many landlords will hire a property management team to manage their buildings and any capital improvement projects. Just like tenant reps and brokers, property managers interact with end users, their "tenants," who are either moving into a building or renewing their lease. They often recommend design teams for their capital improvement projects and for tenant improvement projects going on in their buildings.

Some commercial real estate firms have property management as a service. Some property management firms are independent and offer boutique services to their clients. They are a resource to understand what works in a building and what does not work, since they are responsible for keeping the building up after construction is over. I highly recommend doing a post occupancy survey with your team's property manager or taking them for coffee a few months after the building is up and running to hear what they are finding works well and what could use improvement.

DEVELOPER

Developers bring projects to life from the ground up. They identify potential sites, often working with design teams to evaluate and select the ideal property for development, which can be a lengthy process. Developers work on a wide range of projects, from luxury home communities to office campuses. They have the vision to revitalize communities and the ability to coordinate the necessary resources, teams, and local support to make that vision a reality.

GENERAL CONTRACTOR

General contractors (GCs) build the project. Many GCs "self-perform" work, but most subcontract various aspects of construction, acting as managers for these subcontractors. GCs are responsible for ensuring the project conforms to construction drawings. They manage the construction process and generate RFIs (requests for information), submittals, and pay applications, which document contract performance. The best projects result from excellent working relationships with the design team, the GC team, and the owner.

GCs can be engaged in several ways on a project. In a "design-build" arrangement, the contractor hires the design team to work in tandem to deliver the project. In a CMGC (construction manager general contractor) contract, the GC partners in budget development and invoices the owner for anything outside the scope. In a GMP (guaranteed maximum price) contract, the GC ensures costs do not exceed a set maximum, invoicing the client for anything not included in the drawings.

SUBCONTRACTOR

Subcontractors, whether union or non-union, cover specific areas of the project, such as plumbing, mechanical, electrical, fire protection, flooring, painting, doors, frames, hardware, windows, envelope materials, metal studs, etc. With experience, you will develop a sense of which subcontractors provide the best quality. For example, I prefer working with certain millworkers because of the significant range in quality. When you find reliable subcontractors, you'll want to keep working with them. I recommend asking the GC if they are open to your preferred list of subcontractors in their bidding. Chances are, they know the team you like and are happy to have them onboard.

ENGINEER

Engineers are critical team members to designing a building that performs properly. They produce drawings that detail the building systems, such as structural, mechanical, electrical, plumbing, fire protection, and civil engineering. Depending on your jurisdiction and the preferences of your team, some of these engineers are engaged directly by the GC, and some are under the umbrella of the design team.

By working closely with engineers, we can create well-coordinated designs that showcase the building systems while performing efficiently. For example, if you are going for an open ceiling, industrial look, you will want to review the ducting plan with your mechanical engineer and the wiring plan with your electrical engineer to ensure the routes they take and the look of the ducts and cables match the vision for the project. And every designer knows the pain of having a life safety device that falls in the middle of a feature wall, ruining the feature moment.

Coordinating these devices' placement ahead of time ensures the key design moments are preserved.

FURNITURE REPRESENTATIVE

Furniture reps are salespeople who represent lines of furniture from one or more manufacturers. They are experts in their lines and work with design teams to help with specification questions or showing a client specific furniture pieces before purchase. Once they have specifications from the design team, they provide pricing to a furniture dealer. Furniture is a big business, the politics of which could fill another book. Many designers get into the furniture industry either right out of school or as a career change.

FURNITURE DEALER

Furniture dealers have relationships with multiple furniture lines and have permission to sell that furniture to end users. Not all dealers have relationships with all furniture lines, and some are prohibited from purchasing certain lines. For example, a major furniture manufacturer like Steelcase will have specific preferred dealers. Those dealers make a commitment to Steelcase to sell a certain volume of product per year in exchange for a certain discount structure. Steelcase dealers cannot sell Haworth, MillerKnoll, or Teknion products (or any other large furniture manufacturer competitor). They could potentially still work with those lines, but they would have a "split bid" situation where their specification would be split into multiple packages and distributed to the dealers based on what they could purchase.

Furniture dealers and reps have been incredible allies in my career. They have the benefit of working with every firm in town and know the people and the values of each firm. They can help you find the right fit if you decide to change to a new firm, and they can provide the right introductions. They also have the budget to do business development with designers, and you may find yourself on a private jet headed to Grand Rapids, Milan, or Copenhagen to see products being made firsthand.

PRODUCT REPRESENTATIVE

Products can be everything from paint to hardware to felt to fabric. Every product that goes into a building comes from a manufacturer. Those manufacturers employ sales reps—people who, just like furniture reps, get to know the design community and introduce their products to them in the hopes that they are a good fit for their design projects. Firms often show caution when integrating new products into their projects, as they want quality finishes that will last. If you have an issue with a product, a good product rep can usually help you navigate a resolution.

Furniture reps, dealers, and product reps are well represented in IIDA and ASID. Meeting them through those organizations can be a good way to connect.

BUILDING OFFICIAL

Building officials, or the authorities having jurisdiction (AHJ), such as code enforcement officers, play an integral role in the permitting and regulatory process. Depending on your jurisdiction, the process varies and can change over time based on new or revised laws. In general, every city has a building department that enforces the local building codes and is responsible for the permitting of projects in their area. You may also find that certain cities have regulatory overlays, which means that a certain area of town might have additional regulations or regulatory boards that need to be consulted about your project. For example, the Boston Redevelopment Authority (BRA) has influence over certain areas of Boston, and neighborhood groups like the Fort Point Neighborhood Alliance Commission have influence over parts of the Fort Point neighborhood in Boston. Having a thorough understanding of the local building regulations and processes will be the difference between having your project sail through approvals and being mired down in paperwork and appeals. Take care to understand the people and processes for your jurisdiction to ensure a smooth working relationship.

CONNECTING THE DOTS

There are a few events that bring this intricate and interdependent web of industry colleagues and allies together each year. One of the most anticipated events in New England is the IIDA Fashion Show. Held at a large hotel or convention center, this event is a highlight of the design community calendar, eagerly awaited by all.

Months before the show, local firms partner with furniture and product reps to create masterpiece fashions made from tile, wallcovering, and every other building material you can imagine. The dedication is palpable as teams bond over late nights spent sewing and gluing, working tirelessly to bring their imaginative creations to life. This collaboration fosters a unique synergy both inside and outside the office, strengthening relationships and sparking creativity.

On the night of the event, the atmosphere is electric. Attendees arrive in creative formalwear, buzzing with excitement. A mile-long registration table stands testament to the event's popularity. Elaborate towers of sliders, hors d'oeuvres, and desserts dot the lobby, providing a feast for both the eyes and the palate. Additional bars have been added over the years to cut down on wait times, ensuring everyone has a drink in hand to toast the evening's festivities.

The fashion show itself is nothing short of spectacular. Designs that could rival anything on the catwalk at New York's Fashion Week strut down the runway. The competition is intense, with categories like Best in Show and Most Creative Use of Materials. Past judges have included *Project Runway* winner Christian Siriano and local celebrities, adding prestige to the event. The creativity and craftsmanship on display are truly awe-inspiring, making it clear how much effort each team has invested.

For junior designers, the fashion show is an opportunity to shine on a literal stage at a fun event that attracts a broad cross section of the industry. It's a chance to showcase their creativity, build their networks, and immerse themselves in the vibrant design community. It's a wonderful place to reconnect with people you haven't seen in a while, all while enjoying great food and entertainment. The sense of investment and enthusiasm is contagious, as everyone cheers for their firm and celebrates the hard work that goes into each creation.

The IIDA New England Fashion Show is more than just a competition; it's a celebration of creativity, collaboration, and community. It's events like these that remind us why we love being part of the design industry and inspire us to continue pushing the boundaries of what's possible.

ALLIES TO FRIENDS

The design industry is a whole ecosystem of professionals, each with their part to play in making beautiful spaces tailored to individual clients. You may not see the connections, relationships, or history the people in the industry share when you first join the world of commercial design, but you'll soon get to know them and be part of the story of this dynamic industry. The reality is that we work closely, for long hours, on projects we are wildly passionate about for clients we care about. It is no wonder that many people in the industry find lifelong friends, partners, husbands, and wives from within this community. Let's look at how to navigate those close relationships next.

PART 3

THE GOOD, BAD, AND UGLY OF INDUSTRY RELATIONSHIPS

You know the basics of the culture both inside and outside the firm. Now what happens when your networking starts forming closer relationships?

Here's what's covered about this hot topic in the next few chapters:

→ How to navigate friendships
→ How to navigate dating
→ How to navigate toxic bosses
→ How to find a mentor

CHAPTER 7

FRIENDS

IN THE WORLD OF DESIGN, FRIENDSHIPS CAN BE AS INTE-gral to success as creativity. My own journey in this industry has been profoundly shaped by my friendships. Almost immediately after joining ADD Inc as a full-time designer, I met Tracy. At the time, Tracy and I were newcomers eager to learn the industry. Tracy was transitioning into her second career in design after a successful stint as a hairdresser, balancing her aspirations with the responsibilities of being a single mother. Our instant connection was fueled by a mutual passion for design. We quickly became friends, learning and growing together in those early days. I introduced her to essential design tools like Microstation and, many years later, Canva, while she imparted invaluable life lessons, such as negotiating with difficult roommates.

As we navigated the twists and turns of the design industry and life, our friendship remained a constant. When Tracy's career path led her to a hospitality firm, our bond only strengthened. We supported each other through every season of life—promotions, layoffs, clients, vacations, babies, love, and loss. Our professional achievements mirrored each other's growth, as well, with Tracy becoming the president of the ASID New England chapter, while I took on the role of president of the IIDA New England Chapter. Despite the demands of our careers, we have always remained close. Tracy is my first phone call when something good happens or when I need a pep talk.

Today, Tracy and I both own our own design businesses, and we continue to find ways to collaborate. The trust we have built over the years allows us to seamlessly blend our personal and professional lives, creating a partnership that is both rare and invaluable.

Building such meaningful relationships within the design industry enriches both your professional journey and personal life. The deeper your investment in the people around you, the more profound your experience as a designer will be. Tracy and I are living proof that the connections you cultivate early in your life can become the foundation of a rewarding and enduring career in design.

FRIENDS FOR A REASON

While Tracy and I were destined to be lifelong friends, sometimes it is those who challenge you who teach you the most about yourself and how to work with others. Such was the case with Chloe and Jane, whose rocky start as collaborators ultimately taught them invaluable lessons in their careers.

Chloe was one of the first designers I hired when I was leading interiors at a Boston-based firm. She was polished, well traveled, and genuinely well liked by everyone. Her stellar reputation and impressive portfolio made her an obvious choice for the team. However, it wasn't until I worked with her directly that I discovered the kind, insightful, and talented woman who would become a dear friend.

During my tenure as president of IIDA NE, I sought to build a few committees with talented people who could deliver high-quality programs for the chapter. Chloe was my first choice to run our Design Awards event, one of our marquee chapter events. Given her demanding work schedule, I knew she would need a co-chair. Jane, a well-liked rep who was relatively new to the industry but eager to contribute, seemed like the perfect complement. In my mind, it was a match made in heaven: Chloe, with her extensive industry connections, and Jane, with dedicated work hours for IIDA activities, balanced each other perfectly.

After I introduced them, they began planning the event. A few weeks in, both Chloe and Jane came to me separately, questioning why I thought they would be a good match. Instead of explaining my logic, I asked them, "How is it going?" They each replied that it was a challenge.

We workshopped ways to improve their communication and division of responsibilities, and I checked in periodically. It was tough going. Their management styles clashed, and they had different ideas about presenters. Their working relationship was akin to oil and water. Despite the palpable tension, they remained professional and respectful.

I was perplexed. Why wasn't this match working? I felt guilty for making them uncomfortable, yet I still believed they were the right mix to achieve the best outcome. The night of the event arrived, and I held my breath as I stepped through the door.

The event was flawless. People commented on it being the best awards the chapter had ever seen. While it was little consolation for the discomfort I had caused Chloe and Jane, I hoped they were proud of their accomplishment.

After the event, they handed me a shared card, thanking me for pairing them. I was stunned. They explained that they had grown more from this experience than any other, learning to work with someone different from themselves; respecting each other's ideas, gifts, and styles; and ultimately coming together as a cohesive team. Their journey transformed a challenging partnership into a powerful learning experience.

Their success remains one of my proudest moments. The way they navigated their differences and grew as professionals is a testament to their resilience and dedication. Both Chloe and Jane have gone on to exceptional careers, and I remain in awe of their achievements. Their story is a reminder that sometimes, the most challenging relationships can lead to the most profound growth.

FRIENDS FOR A SEASON

As a junior designer, Chloe was friends with many people—designers, reps, and contractors. She worked hard and eventually became a design manager, bringing in new clients and winning awards. But with her promotion came the challenge of managing some of her friends. This can be tough, even for the most diplomatic person. Friends might feel left out or resentful as you advance. A good friend will cheer you on, but jealousy can strain relationships. If that happens, it's important to address the issue directly. And if things can't be resolved, it might be best to part ways by moving to different teams.

In the design industry, friendships naturally evolve as careers progress. Your relationships might shift as your career takes a different direction. For example, you might move into an ownership role, hiring design teams for a global company's projects. Maintaining professional relationships in this new context is crucial. Or if you transition into a rep role after years as a designer, keeping your connections strong ensures your friends and former colleagues continue using your materials.

If you suddenly find yourself managing people you once partied with, it can be especially hard. Not everyone will be happy for you, even if they should be. Relationships will change—some will last, and some won't.

Most industry friendships are at their closest when you're working together on a project or at the same firm. You might lose touch over time, but those relationships add depth to your career. For instance, I still get texts from my friend Tim, who sends me photos and art of the Federal Reserve building where I got engaged. Even though it's been years since we worked together, I love those reminders of our shared experiences and value his friendship.

Everyone you meet in your career brings something valuable, whether it's a lesson to teach or one to learn. Keep an open mind as you navigate these friendships, and continue learning from those around you.

FRIENDS FOR A LIFETIME

When you are looking back at the end of one phase of your life, and just before the beginning of the next phase, the lessons of your life have a way of clicking together.

When I decided to leave Boston for Portland, Oregon, it was a leap of faith for my family. The news caught people off guard; it felt like stepping into the unknown, but with a deep trust that it would all work out, we jumped.

The design community rallied around me when I shared the decision with friends and colleagues. People came forward with heartfelt stories about how I'd influenced their careers, inspired them to chase their dreams, and helped them to forge lasting connections. Hearing how I'd made a difference was deeply rewarding. It made me feel like my work truly mattered—and isn't that what we all hope for?

As we prepared to leave, I savored every event, client meeting, and moment with my community. Near the end of our time in Boston, I attended one final IIDA event: Art Uncorked. This fundraiser highlighted the diverse artistic talents of our community, from paintings and pottery to sculptures, all auctioned off to support a local charity.

That evening, Ed, Chloe, and Chloe's husband Jack were there. Unbeknownst to me, Chloe was tasked with keeping me at the venue. Jack was busy running the event, while Ed coordinated behind the scenes.

As the event was about to start, I felt cold. "I have to go to my car for a sweater," I told Chloe.

"I'll go with you. Garages can be dangerous," she said, quickly joining me.

"I'm good here," Ed said, waving us off. Despite outward calm, he was sweating bullets, knowing that there was a surprise waiting. He texted Chloe multiple times to hurry back but received no response.

We returned just before Jack took the stage. "Why are you so sweaty?" I asked Ed.

"I'm just hot," he replied. It was sixty-five degrees inside. Thinking it was odd, I turned my attention to the stage as Jack began speaking.

"We want to take a moment at the start of this event to honor someone who has had a significant impact on the industry," he announced.

"Oh," I thought, looking around, "I didn't know we were doing this today."

"Brittney Herrera, come up here!" Jack said, gesturing grandly. "We want to award you with the highest honor we've got, the IIDA New England Leadership Award."

I was stunned and deeply honored. As I walked to the stage,

I was overwhelmed by the recognition from my community. I wasn't planning on speaking that evening, dressed simply in a little black dress and a leopard-print cashmere cardigan. I climbed onto the stage, not sure what was about to come out. "I couldn't have done the things I've done alone. I'm so proud of everything this IIDA community has accomplished together. It takes a dedicated team to have created the change we did, and I know this change will last." I highlighted Jack's work with the communications team, our efforts to build brand awareness, and the positive impact IIDA had on lifting up the Emerging Leaders. I ended with a heartfelt, "I'm going to miss this community."

Receiving the award felt like a goodbye, but thanks to the strong friendships Ed and I had built, it was more of a "see you later." In this industry, when lifelong friendships form, they follow you, no matter how far you go.

LIFELONG BONDS

Tracy, Ed, and I stood in the Chestnut Hill Mall parking lot, just outside a Wegmans grocery store. Fresh from an ultrasound confirming my pregnancy, we shared the news with Tracy about our daughter-to-be.

"I'm so excited for you!" she exclaimed. "This is a big moment!"

Ecstatic, I looked at her smiling face. "Tracy, would you be the baby's godmother?"

The sun blazed down on us. A motley collection of cars and trucks surrounded us, and a clang sounded nearby as a shopper rammed their cart into a corral. It wasn't the ideal setting for such a pivotal life moment. For a brief moment, I worried it might be too much to ask.

I needn't have worried.

"Oh my god, yes!" Tracy cried without hesitation, hugging me tightly. "I'm over the moon right now!"

Friendships in the design industry can become some of the most significant and transformative relationships you will ever experience. Whether they are lifelong bonds like the one I share with Tracy or challenging collaborations that lead to professional growth, each relationship offers valuable lessons and opportunities.

As you navigate your career, your friendships in the industry may evolve. Colleagues integral to your daily life at one point may move in different directions, and your paths may diverge. Maintaining professional relationships becomes crucial, whether you transition to a role on the ownership side, become a rep, or manage people you once considered peers.

Ultimately, the key to thriving in the design industry lies in nurturing these relationships, keeping an open mind, and continuously learning from those around you. By doing so, you not only enhance your professional experience but also enrich your personal life, creating a fulfilling and balanced career.

Of course, sometimes the rules go right out the window, and you end up marrying a colleague.

CHAPTER 8

DATING

I met Ed on my first day at SGA. I was eager to get to know everyone I'd be working with, and when he invited me to an Artists for Humanity party, I was excited to attend. The organization had a space in South Boston, not far from the office. We carpooled with a few other coworkers who were all similar in age and were good friends outside of the office. The party was themed, requiring attendees to dress monochromatically. Ed wore brown. Henry, another architect at the firm, dressed in orange and his wife in bright yellow. I had meetings all day and wore black pants with a silk black camisole and a mottled black-and-gray cardigan. The event staff encouraged me to change my cardigan, pointing to a rack of solid black clothing behind them.

"Absolutely not!" I said.

"But you're going to ruin the photo!" they complained.

"You can photoshop it," I responded dryly. "Gray is a gradient of black, so this color is fine."

The party was fun, and I met my goal of getting to know people, as I made fast friends with Henry's wife. As the night wore on, Ed found me in the crowd and asked, "Do you want to grab dinner? A bunch of us are going."

"Yeah, sounds good," I said, looking to deepen the connections I'd started. "Let's do it."

I met Ed at the door a few minutes later, and as we started walking to the restaurant, I realized there was no one else with us. "They all had other plans," he said, shrugging. I thought that was unusual, since they were all close friends. I found out much later that Ed had told everyone else not to come with us so that he could take me to dinner by himself.

We walked into the Franklin Cafe and grabbed a booth in the back next to a couple who looked like they'd stepped out of *The Sopranos*. Ed and I looked at each other, both thinking the same thing, and had a knowing laugh as we sat down across from one another. We ordered drinks, and as they came, I searched for topics to discuss with my new coworker. He had other plans.

As soon as the drinks landed on our table and our waitress was out of earshot, Ed reached over the table and took my hand dramatically. "What are we going to do about this attraction thing?" he asked, plainly and very seriously.

I was totally caught off guard. "Absolutely nothing," I said emphatically. "We work together!" I added, as though the reason was not obvious.

I loved my new job. My mind was spinning with scenarios. Ed slowly pulled his hand back and acted like nothing had happened as we finished the rest of our now awkward dinner and he walked me to the train to go home alone. I was used to getting hit on, but not this overtly. He made an impression. That was for sure.

The next day, staff had to sit through an HR training video about sexual harassment and dating within a firm. It was hilariously well timed. Ed and I were sitting next to each other pretending that it wasn't the start of something. Henry easily saw beyond our efforts and gave Ed knowing glances through the training.

Ed took me to coffee afterward. "I'm sorry if I made you feel uncomfortable last night," he started. "I didn't think about the potential consequences dating would have on your job and how my advances would make you feel."

"It's really okay," I said, giving him a long pause. I'd had time to marinate on the whole thing overnight, and there was something there. I was still resolved to make my new role my priority, and not a relationship. As we headed out of the coffee shop, I said, "Not that it wouldn't be nice."

DATING GONE WRONG

Dating in the design industry is common. It happens when people are working side by side on intense creative projects, attending conferences together, or traveling to project sites. Like all relationships, some work out and some don't. I recommend that you familiarize yourself with any official policies your firm may have around dating.

Gina and I started at our firm around the same time. She had a wholesome, warm quality that drew people in, and she came to the firm from a reputable design school. People loved working with her. Gina started secretly dating John, a senior leader at an engineering company that our firm worked with frequently. He was handsome and well liked in the industry. John was unmarried and, as far as we knew, hadn't dated anyone in the industry until Gina. They tried to make it work, but they were both under a microscope in demanding careers. The relationship was short lived but became the talk of the town once people caught on.

If you decide to date someone in the industry, be aware that it could be awkward if it doesn't work out, and your coworkers may feel caught in the middle of the drama.

I also had a secret work relationship that didn't quite work out. He was a talented architect at the firm, designing creative projects throughout New England. He rode motorcycles, lived in a renovated historic building, and had a "cool guy" edge that was softened by his love of cats. Not even our closest friends knew we were together. He had recently ended an engagement and wasn't looking to jump into a serious relationship.

We had just stopped dating when the firm called an all-hands meeting one morning. For this meeting, I'd managed to get a good spot, visible to everyone lining the walls and sitting in the chairs in the firm's common area. "It saddens us to report that Graham died in a motor vehicle accident yesterday," the leaders said solemnly. "We'll keep you all informed when and where the service will be. If anyone wants to talk, please reach out."

I think I made a small noise before I blacked out, right in the middle of everyone, who now all knew Graham and I had been more than just coworkers. I had no warning, and being informed in such an impersonal way was traumatizing. I managed to make my way back to my desk, but I don't remember how. I tried to continue with my work; I didn't know what else to do. Everyone else was dealing with their own pain at the news. Someone they'd known and worked alongside for years had just died suddenly and tragically, and now they knew someone else they worked with had been dating him in secret. That's a lot to take in all at once. But everyone was kind and gentle with me after that, and in an odd way, the whole situation made people more curious about me.

Things happen, and you can't always predict or prepare for how a relationship will affect you or the firm culture around you. People were kind to me after my relationship ended in dramatic fashion. No matter how much you want to keep a relationship secret until you know if it's going to turn out okay, there are always ways it comes to light.

Romance doesn't just happen with lower-level employees. Sometimes the leaders in a firm also form romantic entanglements, and if the relationship is complicated or goes south, the whole firm can suffer. I've witnessed several instances where my bosses dated. Sometimes the relationship is out in the open. Sometimes it is not.

In one case, Jen, one of the principals at a large firm, was known for making people redo work at the last minute and for making decisions that seemed to lead to budget overages. She would sometimes insert herself into projects where she didn't need to be.

In one spectacular example, she lost a big project for the office. I had gotten a call to interview for the project while she was on vacation. I went to the interview and immediately connected with the client, winning the project.

When Jen came back from vacation, she called my desk and asked for the contact information for the client. I reluctantly gave it to her, sensing an issue, but she was my boss, and there was not much I could do to stop her. She called them and said, "I'm so glad to be back from vacation so I can take over as the principal in charge of the project we're doing together!"

The client was not impressed. "We hired a specific team, and you weren't on it," they said. Then they fired the firm and went with someone else.

The broker who had recommended us for the project called me to say how disappointed he was. "I'm surprised a principal did that; it's never happened before."

George, the principal in charge of the firm's office, had taken me under his wing, so I counted him as a trustworthy mentor.

"I'm having trouble with Jen," I said one day in his office. "What advice can you give me for working with her?" I thought the question was diplomatic enough, but the response I got was cold.

"I'm not sure I'm the one to help you mend this fence," he said dismissively. "But you'd better figure it out if you want to be successful here."

I felt like I had crossed a line I didn't know existed.

It turned out that George and Jen were dating. They had kept their relationship a secret. If I'd known this information beforehand, I would have known my approach wasn't going to go anywhere, and I could have looked for other avenues, like moving teams. Winning and then losing that project due to office politics was one of my catalysts for leaving that firm.

Relationships affect firm culture, both at the micro and macro levels, and those relationships can be hard to navigate if they are opaque. If a complicated relationship goes high enough, it won't just affect teams and departments; it will affect the whole firm. Accountability can be difficult to enforce in those situations, and you may find it is easier to move on to a firm that doesn't come with those complications.

Navigating romantic relationships in the design industry requires careful consideration. While some relationships, like those I've witnessed, can lead to interoffice challenges and even damage professional reputations, others can offer profound support and partnership. Now we will explore examples of when workplace romances go right, leading to lifelong partnerships and marriages that enhance both personal and professional lives.

DATING GONE RIGHT

The relationship wasn't hard to hide. No one noticed when Ed and I slipped out for coffee every day, exchanged innocent text messages, and found excuses to hang out after work. Only Ed's close friends suspected, but for the most part, we flew under the radar as we got to know each other.

It was a whirlwind, complicated by the fact that I was living with my then-boyfriend and several roommates in Cambridge. My friends had begged me not to marry him, and our relationship was on life support. He encouraged me to spend time with colleagues to integrate into the firm's culture since work was important to him, as well, but I knew it was over with him the minute Ed grabbed my hand at the Franklin Cafe.

As we prepared to leave for the Design Awards, an event where Ed would meet many of my friends and former colleagues, I knew it was time to tell Ed about my boyfriend. We had been getting to know each other for a few weeks by then and wanted to take things further. I didn't want any surprises at the event, as it was the first time we would be meeting some of my friends and former coworkers together, so I asked Ed to meet me at The Times, a bar across the street from the office. Nervous but determined, I walked into the bar and saw Ed sitting with a pint in hand.

"I have something I need to tell you," I blurted, standing beside him. "I have a boyfriend. We live together." I held my breath, waiting for his reaction. He broke the silence with a broad smile and a big laugh. Confused, I asked, "What's so funny?"

"I'm married," Ed said with an ironic smile. Relief washed over me as he quickly added that he was separated and in the process of getting a divorce. We laughed together about the absurdity of it all and left for the event together, lighter having shared our secrets.

You never know where you're going to find love.

While there are many reasons not to get involved with a coworker, it happens. And there are many people who are happily married within the industry. Designers marry reps. Reps marry each other. Designers marry across their firm or marry designers at other firms. I have seen almost every permutation of successful matches and remarkably low divorce rates. I only know two industry couples who have gotten divorced. While I am sure there must be others, that should tell you how rare it is.

Before we were married, Ed and I maintained healthy boundaries at the office. We escaped for the occasional midday coffee date, but as anyone in the field knows, the pace of a design firm is fast, and the hours are long. When one of us was on a deadline and the other wasn't, there was a deep understanding and respect for what the other was dealing with at that moment, and we didn't have to explain why it was important or feel guilty for taking the time. It was liberating to be with someone who just "got it."

There are other benefits to dating within the industry beyond having an understanding partner. You may also find that you have a more understanding boss. For example, Jerry, an architect, and Veronica, an administrative assistant, were married with two kids, and both worked in the same small office.

When our boss needed them to work late, it was obvious that he had to choose one of them, not both. This helped maintain balance for them and helped our boss gain perspective on the fact that everyone had responsibilities outside the office. Jerry would stay late when we had a drawing deadline, and Veronica would stay late when we had billing or a proposal due. Jerry and Veronica's arrangement allowed them to manage their home life better, ensuring that one of them was always available for their children, pets, and household duties.

Having a partner who gets it is invaluable. It means having

someone who understands the unique pressures and joys of the industry, someone who can empathize with the late nights and celebrate the project wins. It means having someone who can share both your professional and personal life, creating a balance that is supportive and fulfilling.

KEEPING BOUNDARIES

Not everyone respects boundaries or takes a gentle hint when you're not interested in dating. This can be awkward, or at times, feel dangerous.

As part of my job, I do a lot of business development. That usually involves going out for meals or golfing with brokers, developers, contractors, reps, and property managers. Most of them I count as friends. With some, I keep my distance. As you develop relationships with industry professionals, you will learn to follow your gut when it comes to who you can trust and who you can't.

A new development was going in near Government Center, and I had an informal meeting with the project lead from the developer. A mutual industry friend had introduced us, and my firm was bidding on the project, worth millions in fees. Adam and I had not crossed paths before, but I had heard his name mentioned from time to time, associated with various buildings around town.

He invited me out to the Omni Parker House, a touristy choice but close to my office at the time. Despite its proximity, I had never been there except to drop off friends and family visiting from Maine. I walked into the historic lobby and found my way to the bar.

After one drink, he asked, "Do you want to get a room with me?"

I almost laughed until I looked up and found he was serious. "No thank you," I said politely and tried to steer the conversation back to work.

A few sips later, he asked, "No, seriously, do you want to get a room?"

"No. I have a boyfriend," I said, thinking that would end it like it normally did.

"I don't care," he pushed.

Refraining from rolling my eyes, I smiled and quipped back, "It matters to me." Humor was better than getting angry to defuse the situation. I might have to work with him, if not on this project, then on others. Maintaining a relationship, especially with someone so connected to others in my network, felt professionally important in the moment.

He asked about eight more times, and each time I found another polite way to refuse. I was counting the seconds and searching for an excuse to elegantly end our conversation.

All of a sudden, I heard a loud "ahem" as an older woman next to us cleared her throat. She looked like a grandmother on vacation in the big city, with her best friend sitting next to her in their ladies-who-lunch hats. She angled toward our table and looked down her patrician nose at Adam.

"Yes?" Adam said.

"I feel like I'm on an episode of *What Would You Do?* with John Quiñones," she said, "and a camera is going to come out any second because the young lady has obviously said no."

Well, John Quiñones did not pop out. We were not on a TV show. I thought I was deflecting like a champion while maintaining a working relationship for the future. We were almost through the last drink when I would excuse myself to catch my train. But after my good Samaritan called him out, Adam immediately ended things and left. Adam called to apologize the next day, but the project went to our competition, and I never saw him again.

This kind of situation can happen to anyone when there is a power dynamic at play. If you experience an unwanted come-on, either from coworkers or other industry folks, my recommendation is to communicate your boundaries firmly. If you know that you will encounter them again, bring a colleague. I hope that we are evolving out of this kind of toxic dynamic, but it's important to let you know that these situations happen and you should be prepared to handle them in a way that feels right to you.

There will always be another project. Don't be afraid to stand up for yourself.

BALANCING RELATIONSHIPS

In navigating relationships within the industry, it's crucial to cultivate meaningful friendships, understand the dynamics of dating coworkers, and maintain firm boundaries. Friendships can lead to strong professional networks, while dating someone who understands the industry's demands can be incredibly supportive. However, always ensure boundaries are respected to safeguard your personal and professional integrity. Balancing these aspects can lead to a fulfilling and harmonious work-life experience.

CHAPTER 9

SURVIVING TOXIC BOSSES

NOAH WAS A KEY FIGURE AT THE FIRM, EXPERTLY MANAG-ing projects for landlords with multiple buildings where tenants frequently moved in and out. These landlord-driven tenant improvement projects involved documenting renovations for new tenants at a fixed cost. Although junior designers often see these projects as less creative—since they must adhere to existing design standards—they provide an incredible foundation for learning. Through these projects, I learned how to assemble comprehensive drawing sets, specify economical materials, and meet tight deadlines. These projects were also highly profitable for the firm, billed based on the square footage of the space being renovated, with swift turnaround times. Noah's proficiency in handling these projects made him an essential asset to the firm.

When I was first assigned to work with Noah, I didn't realize what a valuable experience it would be. I didn't yet appreciate his role as a mentor or understand how crucial these projects were to the firm's success. Over time, I came to see Noah not just as a project lead but as a patient teacher who was dedicated to helping me grow. Under his guidance, I spent a year balancing five to ten tenant improvement projects each week. It was challenging, but it was also an exceptional learning opportunity that taught me the nuts and bolts of running a successful project.

When the time came for me to move on from working with Noah, I felt a mix of gratitude and eagerness. I was excited to take what I had learned and apply it to new and diverse projects, collaborating with more team members and exploring different facets of design. Noah had equipped me with the tools and knowledge needed to tackle more complex and high-profile projects, and I was ready for the next step in my career.

The opportunities that followed were exhilarating. I worked on projects that garnered awards and were featured in trade magazines. The skills I honed under Noah's mentorship became the cornerstone of my success, not only as a team member but also in establishing my own practice.

Navigating different roles and mentors is an essential part of growth in any firm. Instead of focusing solely on what's challenging, consider how each experience can contribute to your professional development. How can these opportunities help you sharpen your skills and advance your career? And how do you know when it's time to embrace new challenges? This chapter offers insights to help you answer these questions and navigate your career path more effectively.

NAVIGATING TOXIC LEADERSHIP

At one point in my career, I was once presented with an opportunity to pivot into multifamily projects at a new firm. Excited by the chance to work in this vertical, I was eager to make the shift. However, shortly after joining, the project I was hired for was unexpectedly put on hold due to funding issues. With that door temporarily closed, I found myself working on healthcare projects instead—an area that, while interesting, wasn't my primary passion.

Adjusting to this new firm and new vertical was more challenging than I had anticipated. The pace was slower, and the office dynamics were more complex than I was used to, which left me feeling unsettled. To keep myself engaged and continue growing, I sought opportunities outside the office. I began teaching at the Boston Architectural College (BAC), where I could share my knowledge and stay connected to the next generation of designers. Additionally, I joined the board of the International Interior Design Association (IIDA) as the director of students, which allowed me to engage with the broader design community and build a network of supportive peers.

Despite these fulfilling activities, the dynamics at the firm remained challenging. Leadership styles varied significantly, leading to frequent clashes and a tense work environment. Junior designers often felt like they were walking on eggshells, caught in the middle of conflicting directives from different leaders. Feedback sessions, which should have been constructive, often turned into unproductive critiques that stifled creativity and morale. Instead of fostering a culture of growth, the atmosphere became one where people were more focused on avoiding conflict than on doing their best work.

In an attempt to manage these tensions, the firm experimented with different approaches, including suggesting that employees attend conflict resolution sessions together. I found myself in one such session with a colleague over workload disagreements. While the effort was meant to improve communication, it often felt more like a band-aid solution rather than addressing the underlying issues.

Fortunately, I found an ally in Julia, a talented designer who had a knack for navigating the firm's politics. Together, we supported each other. However, even with Julia's support, the constant stress and toxic culture began to take a toll on my health. It was a wakeup call to realize how much a negative work environment could affect my physical and mental well-being.

As the situation became increasingly untenable, I knew I needed to make a change. It was clear that staying in an environment where I couldn't produce my best work or maintain my well-being was not sustainable.

To be clear, other people thrived in this firm—they had a deep network of colleagues, fulfilling work in a vertical they aligned with, and a history of coming up in the industry with their peers there.

Everyone has a different experience within a firm. One person's idea of a perfect firm may not align with someone else's ideal. Deciding to leave a job is a deeply personal decision that involves weighing the benefits of staying against the costs to your health, happiness, and professional growth. If you find yourself in a similar situation, it's important to recognize the signs and consider whether it might be time to seek out a new environment—one that allows you to thrive instead of just survive.

FINDING FULFILLMENT BEYOND THE OFFICE

At the time, there was a recession, and I wasn't in a place where I felt comfortable quitting the firm without another position lined up. I was searching for a new firm, but options were limited. I stayed busy with my volunteer work and slowly started to build my connections.

Teaching at the BAC was hugely rewarding. My students were amazing people who, at times, taught more than I taught them. I led a section of Design Principles and Foundation A Studio in the beginning, focusing on the fundamentals of design for first-year students. There were other sections led by colleagues from other firms, and we collaborated to reimagine the curriculum. Tina Blythe taught some of the faculty as part of a Design Education certification program, which I soaked in. Eventually I went on to teach Residential and Commercial Design Studios as well.

When I wasn't teaching, IIDA filled the balance of my time with industry events, student outreach, and board duties. The overlap of my teaching role and my tenure as director of students made for synergies as I did outreach to local universities. When it came time to host Portfolio Day, the BAC provided a wonderful venue for the event in Cascieri Hall. Membership was up, and people had a positive outlook on IIDA and the value of membership.

My work with IIDA did not go unnoticed. Little did I know that I had the attention of my colleagues, and as people started to hire, my name was floated around as a potential candidate. When I got the call to interview at SGA, I was relieved. When I learned it came from a board connection, I was elated that my network had come through for me in this way.

How you handle adversity can define your success. While I do not advocate for staying in toxic situations, I do advocate for evaluating the situation, seeing if there is anything you can do to make it better or to learn from it, and strategically choosing to move on if that is the right path for you. And when your options are limited, do what you can to find fulfilling ways to contribute to organizations that share your values.

NAVIGATING WORK-LIFE BALANCE IN
A DEMANDING ENVIRONMENT

One day, I was called into a conference room for an unexpected meeting. The senior leader of my team, a seasoned architect with a significant influence in the firm, closed the door and asked me to sit. "This firm isn't set up for people with family commitments," he stated flatly, his tone leaving no room for interpretation. His words caught me off guard. I believed I was performing well and contributing positively to the team's success. This senior leader had a family of his own, so I had assumed that family values were inherent to the firm's culture. Besides, I hadn't yet shared that I was pregnant, as it was still early in my pregnancy.

His comment hung in the air, and as I started to respond, he interrupted, continuing, "I expect you to stay at the office whenever your team is working late. I hope that's clear." Without waiting for a response, he abruptly left the room, leaving me to process the sudden shift in tone. I realized he was frustrated because I had gone home after completing my tasks while the rest of the team stayed late to finalize a presentation. Given the limitations of the software we were using, only one person could work on the document at a time. I had checked in with my team before leaving to ensure there was nothing more I could do to help. However, I soon learned that the unwritten rule was to stay in the office as long as any part of the team was still there.

This reprimand came out of nowhere. Up until that point, I had been successfully bringing in significant business and was even seen as a rising star in the firm. My work habits hadn't been questioned before, and the sudden critique felt both confusing and unfair. This incident became a turning point for me—a catalyst to seek out a workplace where my ability to balance professional responsibilities and family commitments would be appreciated and respected.

As my pregnancy progressed, it became increasingly clear that my time at the firm was limited. Other mothers at the firm began to approach me, sharing their own experiences. When my condition finally caught the attention of the senior leader, his reaction was tepid at best. A colleague prompted him, saying, "Look. Brittney is expecting! Isn't that wonderful?" His response was a curt "Congratulations," with little enthusiasm or acknowledgment of the situation.

Before I left the firm, I shared my experiences with a trusted colleague, highlighting not just my personal challenges but also the broader implications for the team. "It doesn't matter to me now because I'm leaving," I explained, "but this is affecting the whole team."

Interestingly, after my departure, I heard from a friend still at the firm that they had begun to implement more flexible policies regarding family commitments. She felt better supported when it came time for her own family planning, noticing a shift toward more accommodating work hours and a more understanding attitude about balancing work and family life. This kind of change is often driven by necessity—when firms see a dip in revenue or a talent drain, they become more open to adjusting their policies to stay competitive. Those that don't adapt risk losing relevance in a rapidly evolving market. While some firms that resist change struggle to survive, others that embrace it continue to thrive.

TAKING THE GOOD WITH THE BAD

Now that I lead a firm, I empathize with my former bosses in ways I never could have before. Seeing them as more human,

I can forgive their mistakes and appreciate the lessons they inadvertently taught me about the kind of leader I wanted to be. They prompted me to read extensively on managing people, navigating office dynamics, and improving myself. I wouldn't trade these lessons for anything.

Everyone makes mistakes, even at the top. There will always be moments when the dream job turns into a nightmare. Yet from even the harshest situations, unexpected lessons can emerge. Don't be afraid to get creative when facing challenges. Seek allies who can advocate for you in places where you can't speak for yourself.

Opportunities abound, even in challenging environments. They might come from within your current firm or from the broader industry. Building a professional network can create exit ramps when you need them; you just have to be ready to take those opportunities.

A firm leader who genuinely invites feedback and works to improve the culture is ideal but not universal. Even in a firm that values feedback, no one is perfect all the time. Leaders have bad days and stressors like anyone else, which can lead to negative interactions. Sometimes, what feels like a punishment might stem from a misunderstanding. In such cases, resisting might only worsen the situation. It's often better to navigate the challenge, demonstrating resilience and capability through your actions.

Mistakes are opportunities for growth for everyone. As a junior designer, you can influence your firm positively by incorporating the good practices you've seen elsewhere. No experience is wasted. You learn what to do—and what not to do—from every firm you work at. Every boss has something to teach you, even those who seem out of touch. I took the good from every boss I ever had to create Thunder Egg, a place where people are valued and can grow, make mistakes, and reach their full potential. I work every day to ensure it stays that way. I'm not perfect, but I had excellent teachers along the way.

IT'S UP TO YOU

Navigating challenging bosses and challenging work environments is part of the professional journey. Learn from every experience. Seek out positive influences, and remember that you have the power to shape your career and the culture around you. Embrace the lessons, and build your network. Strive to create a positive environment wherever you go.

CHAPTER 10

MENTORS

NINA HAD HEARD FROM AN ASSOCIATE PRINCIPAL THAT I was underperforming. We'd had a miscommunication on how she wanted a drawing done, and she'd assumed that I had done it wrong on purpose or that I was incompetent—neither was true, of course. However, when I was moved onto Nina's team, it felt like she, and everyone else, was waiting for me to make a mistake.

"Where are the files I asked you to save?" she said, urgently walking into my desk area.

I blinked in surprise at her tone, a spike of panic shooting through me. Had I messed up again? Had I put them in the wrong place? Was this the last straw and now I'd get fired? A few clicks of the mouse, and relief spread through me, "They're right here in the folder you told me to put them in," I said, showing her my screen.

Nina's face relaxed when she saw the offending files, right where they were supposed to be. "I'm so sorry. I must have missed them." She knew she'd messed up, frightened me unnecessarily, all because she'd been expecting the worst.

Nina's small mistake shifted her whole perspective on me

and how I'd been treated in the firm up until that point. She became one of my biggest advocates. Once people understood that I had Nina in my corner, people opened up, and my past missteps were left in the past.

A good advocate will speak up for you when you're not in the room and will advise you on what you can do to help navigate the politics of your firm. Your number-one task when starting at a new firm is to get an advocate on the leadership team. If no one knows you, they can't advocate for you to get choice jobs, go to bat for you come raise time, or help you make it through layoffs in the down times. The more invaluable you are, the more leaders in the firm will want you to continue to thrive.

FORMAL ADVISORS

Hopefully, you find yourself in a firm with a good mentorship program and are assigned an advisor who will help you navigate your new firm as well as the initial stages of your career. Formal advising programs typically have defined metrics for success within a given role or title. They track your progress in achieving licensure or accreditation. Many also track soft skills like how you get along with clients and colleagues. I heard once that a popular private equity firm records its employees' conversations at all times, and staff rate how they make each other feel and how they are performing in real time. That is extreme, but you should know that everything you do at the firm will color how you do on your performance review.

ADD Inc had an excellent advising program. It was also one of the few firms that was employee owned. This attracted entrepreneurial talent, and the whole firm had a "we are in this together" vibe. The structure of ADD Inc set the table for a good mentorship experience. Everybody was invested in your growth. They were also invested in quickly rehabilitating you if you were underperforming. They only wanted to work with the best. It made us junior designers stretch and grow faster and further than we would have at a firm that didn't care to look over our shoulders, hold us accountable to transparent performance standards, and validate when we did well.

Megan was my advisor, and she was wonderful at guiding me through the firm. Goals included general tasks like creating a timeline for passing the National Council for Interior Design Qualifications (NCIDQ) and personal tasks to elevate my standing in the firm. I felt I had some repair to do after my misstep with the associate principal, so Megan advocated for me to be involved in planning the firm's annual ski trip. She had me develop training for Leadership in Energy and Environmental Design (LEED) certification after seeing my highly organized study guide. People started coming to me whenever they wanted to get certified. By the end of my goal-setting and goal-achieving period, I was highly credentialed and well regarded in the firm. I even won employee of the month.

Megan also helped me navigate my compensation. She helped me understand where I was in relation to what other people were making annually, giving me the range based on her experience. That's part of a mentor's job too: giving you information to understand where you are on the bell curve of industry salaries for your level and where you need to be, which can give you the confidence to ask for what you're worth in the next salary negotiation cycle.

My mentor didn't just advocate for my compensation. She also advocated for my reputation. When I was with a team I wasn't gelling with, she encouraged me to keep going. "Do the things they're asking you to do, and as soon as we can move you on to another team, we will," she told me. It was easier to endure when I knew she was championing me behind the scenes. She also didn't offer to rescue me by getting me out immediately, allowing me to take ownership of rescuing myself. Instead, she supported me by drawing attention to my wins.

Megan wasn't just an advisor; she was an example to follow. She was well liked at the firm and had a positive outlook on life. When we met, she was pregnant with her first child, and she became an example of how to balance motherhood and firm life.

One of the few downsides to formal mentorships is their randomness and, often, their time limit. My first mentor at ADD Inc happened to be a gem and really good for me, but my second was the total opposite. Each advisor was assigned to each advisee for three years before rotating to the next person. While this strategy helped spread the senior designers' experience and skill sets, it was hard to let go of a good advisor. It was also hard if the next advisor who rotated in was a bad one, since not all the senior designers wanted or had the personality to be good teachers. My second advisor took no interest in me. He checked the boxes for my goal-setting and evaluations and then said, "Have a nice day," on his way out the door.

Lacking direction, I went back to Megan to ask what I should do. "He's a principal," she said, shrugging. "It's not worth arguing for a change because you don't want to take the risk of ruffling his feathers, which could limit your ability to grow in the firm. My advice? Wait it out. Another person will rotate in before you know it."

Eventually, I wanted to pivot from workplace design into multifamily residential—I loved the space planning challenge of laying out units and working through complex systems in the drawings. However, it proved to be too much of a change for the firm, and with no advocate in my corner, my request was denied. I left the firm shortly after.

A good advocate can make or break your career. If you find that you don't have a good formal advisor, it's time to find an informal one.

INFORMAL ADVISORS

The idea of mentoring in the moment is a powerful and effective way to learn. Getting feedback in real time helps you to course correct with examples of where you need to improve and guidance on how to do so.

When I was working on a project for a global tech company, we had a large team of designers responsible for 500,000 square feet of office space. The floors were enormous, and working through a presentation on the project took a fair amount of time. Part of my job in the design phase was to assist with the overall layout and to develop and communicate the finishes and furniture.

Evan was our design lead on the project. He was an admired designer and had a wonderful flair for delivering a presentation so the client was excited for the end product. He also turned out to be an excellent mentor on the job. Through the process, Evan acted as my editor, making changes where he needed to in order to make everything perfect.

He'd also make me practice my presentation skills. For various aspects of the design, he'd put me on the spot. "Okay, sell me," he'd say, crossing his arms and waiting.

Oh, that's what we're doing? I thought. I stumbled through at first but then realized that this was excellent practice. Soon I could convince him of even the bits he initially vetoed. That practice helped me to become a confident presenter of my work.

As soon as we were out of the design phase for the interiors, I took on the furniture for the entire space. I burned through the task, creating a layout, choosing pieces, integrating standards, selecting alternates, and creating a spreadsheet for estimated budgeting, and then I presented it to the client. We got full approval, sailing through the presentation and setting new standards for them into the future.

Now that I knew I could ask for and get feedback in real time, I took the opportunity to ask our project leader what I could have done better in our presentation. She was quick to say, "Nothing. It went really well." But I could hear her thinking as she paused afterward and then said, "Well, you could limit the use of manufacturer names with clients—they don't know who they are anyway, and it comes off as too in the weeds." That kind of fine-tuning helped me to become an even better presenter.

One of the most significant mentors in my career was James. James taught me an enormous amount about the industry, running a firm, and listening to clients. While the firm didn't have a formal advising program when I started there, James acted as a dedicated mentor from the time I was hired until I left five years later.

James's mentorship covered every aspect of the business: how to run a firm, network with clients and industry colleagues, read a contract, write a proposal, track KPIs (key performance indicators), win work, efficiently do the work, effectively write an additional service letter, design with a clear process, hold clients accountable, fire a client, handle being fired by a client gracefully, manage teams, hire people, let people go, put together a strong team, motivate people, and let others shine. Each lesson was imparted through direct involvement and real-world examples, making the learning process both rigorous and rewarding.

We had a long streak of winning work—it was a golden time of expansion when office leases were in demand and high-profile companies were flocking to the area, and our team had something special. Relationships that James had laid the groundwork for were starting to pay off, and the firm's profile was rising.

We would have long days of early meetings, design charrettes, interviews, drinks after work, and industry events in the evening. Both of us were running on empty after months of this pace, but I loved it.

I took the first pass at proposals and interview decks, and I would get them back with redlines over every page, layer upon layer of feedback. Even small details, like how a sentence was worded, were under review. I would fold in the edits and take it back for another round of redlines. Sometimes three or four rounds later, we would have a final draft. I never took it personally, but the day that I got back a clean proposal with no redlines on it was a memorable day indeed!

The same was true of any documentation sets. The redlines, missing details, dimensioning strategy, labels, sheet organization—everything was subject to redlines. Eventually, we had a template with a checklist that helped us get through with minimal markups, leading to greater efficiency and greater project profitability.

We won industry awards for our work designing spaces for several tech companies. Soon, we were traveling to other parts of the country to do design work. Eventually, I was bringing in projects through the connections I had developed while at the firm, earning bonuses for some.

One day, I was working on a large project in the Seaport, and it was going well…or so I thought, until James came over and sat down. He had a small smile and kind eyes as he said, "I have good news and I have bad news. The bad news is that the client has asked that you be taken off the project." I reeled. What? Did I hear him right? Was I going to be fired for this? How did this happen? James went on, "The good news is that this happens to everyone at one point or another, and now it has happened to you." I stared at him as my mind worked to catch up. It sounded like I still had a job. Okay, that was good. But why did the client fire me? It took me some time and deep reflection to come up with a theory, but ultimately, not every personality meshes with each other.

James was kind in how he broke this news, and he was supportive as I worked to listen better to the client's tone and needs. I went on to work behind the scenes on the job while the senior project manager on my team wrapped things up at the client site.

My time at the firm was pivotal on many levels. James's mentorship was instrumental in shaping my approach to design, client interactions, and leadership. The connections I formed and the lessons I learned continue to influence my career. I work with firm alumni to this day, and they are some of the most talented, professional, dedicated people I have met. It's an honor to be one of them!

THE POWER OF MENTORS

One day, sitting across from Nina, I overheard her on a conference call with a client. She promised them that we would follow up after the meeting with the necessary files. Hearing this, I quickly emailed her the files, enabling her to deliver a quick win in her meeting.

Being proactive and helping a colleague to look good builds trust in a team. We still talk about that story as an example of being in sync and able to rely on each other. Nina also taught me to use "we" instead of "I" when representing the firm, an important distinction that underscores the value of teamwork.

Nina knew I had her back, and she had mine.

Having a mentor or advocate is not just about having someone to guide you; it's about having someone who believes in you, supports you, and helps you navigate the challenges of your career. A good advocate can open doors, provide opportunities, and give you the confidence to take risks and pursue your goals.

When I look back on my career, I can see the impact that my mentors and advocates have had. They have been there to support me, challenge me, and help me grow. They have taught me valuable lessons, given me the tools to succeed, and helped me to become the professional I am today.

As you grow in your career, it's important to also give back and become a mentor to others. By sharing your knowledge and experience, you can help the next generation of designers to succeed and continue the cycle of mentorship and advocacy.

Finding and nurturing relationships with mentors and advisors is one of the most important things you can do for your career. These relationships will provide you with guidance, support, and opportunities, helping you to grow and succeed in your chosen field So, take the time to seek out mentors, build strong relationships, and give back by mentoring others. The rewards will be immeasurable.

PART 4

STAR POWER

You've done the work to build your community in the design industry. Now it's time to hone your skills and step into your potential as a leader.

In the following chapters, you'll learn:

→ How to identify the traits of a star
→ How to grow your leadership skills in safe places
→ How to plan for your next five years

CHAPTER 11

STAR POWER

WHEN I JOINED A GLOBAL FIRM AS A DESIGN DIRECTOR, everything changed. It felt like stepping from the shadows into the spotlight. My network—reps, colleagues, engineers, furniture dealers, and brokers—responded with newfound enthusiasm and support.

Clients trusted that I would understand their needs and deliver solutions that fit their budgets and schedules. My reputation for being easy to work with and providing customized solutions had already attracted significant clients, which ultimately brought me to the firm's doorstep.

Now that you've laid the groundwork and secured a mentor to guide you through the complexities ahead, it's time to focus on what makes a designer truly stand out. Building your personal brand is key—it's what will set you apart from the crowd and attract the right people and opportunities like a magnet.

STARS KNOW IT'S NOT ABOUT THEM

James and I would visit local universities to meet graduating interior designers and answer questions they had about the profession, IIDA, or the firm. At the time, James was the sitting president of IIDA New England, and I was the director of students for the chapter. I described my career path to the students, detailing how my network and IIDA played an important role in getting a great job with a great team. My primary piece of advice was to shift their perspectives from themselves to the firm.

That subtle shift is powerful. It demonstrates to your interviewer and then to the team you join that you are in it together and that you will do what it takes to win together.

As you have gathered by now, developing leads, bidding, and winning new work is time intensive, and in a competitive field, business development can be a full-time job. When a junior designer comes to meet a client and they put them off and lose the project, it is crushing for the person who developed that opportunity. Firm leaders want to hire people who understand and value the relationships they have spent years fostering. They want staff who will take care of their clients. So show them you care about the firm's goals and you are a team player.

STARS HOLD THE VISION

When it was my turn to take on the role of president of IIDA New England, not all the changes made during my tenure were welcomed by select members of our community. Some changes even angered a few people. As part of our overhaul on chapter communications, we launched a newsletter called *The Wire* that pulled industry happenings, announcements, and trends together in one place. There was an op-ed column that was led by a talented designer who was just finding his voice as a trendsetter.

Most people loved it. The column tracked trends, opined on happenings in the industry, and gave designers a relatable editorial that made them feel seen.

I was caught off guard when I received an angry phone call from a chapter sponsor. He said that he felt that IIDA was no place for a political agenda and that as a key donor, he wanted the op-ed section of *The Wire* removed. I was surprised, as I hadn't seen anything political about the content of the column.

As a chapter, we were fostering an environment of inclusion and raising up the voices of promising junior designers. *The Wire* and the op-ed in particular provided a platform for relevant topics in the industry. Censoring those topics felt wrong. I told the donor that I would not be censoring our communications team.

You won't always please everyone. Stay true to the vision that you and your organization have set. Filter all feedback through the lens of whether it aligns with the vision. As you develop and stretch into leadership roles, being the keeper of the vision becomes an important success metric.

When you need to push back, remember, whether it is in a firm or in a professional organization, you are building a community. Be diplomatic with your feedback. Build an understanding for why you may be rejecting feedback, and tie it to a larger goal for context. Try to understand the other person's point of view—especially if it is hard. It might help you to fine-tune messaging and galvanize the community rather than dividing it.

STARS KEEP A POSITIVE ATTITUDE

I don't know who first said it first, but I've always liked the phrase "Why is this happening *for* me?" instead of "Why is this happening *to* me?"

Sometimes being in a difficult situation can be the best thing for you because it will force you to grow. I know I grew every time I faced a challenge. Now, when I am thrown a curveball, I immediately work to reframe it, which takes the panic out of the situation, replacing it with curiosity and action.

When I was designing the headquarters for a software company in a high-demand Boston neighborhood, we had a design meeting to review the extensive environmental branding scope and a preliminary "look and feel" review of the furniture. The meeting was brief since we were just going over updates to the package that folded in the clients' previous comments. When we were done, one of the stakeholders was fuming. He felt the meeting was a waste of time and that we should have had more for them to review that day. I was shocked, and I apologized for miscommunicating the agenda and reassured him that the items covered would help us to efficiently wrap up the design. He quipped that the company deserved better, and I could see that there was no saving the situation, so I responded with a sincere apology and let it hang in the air, offering no more fodder for him to use in his rage.

After he left, his colleague apologized for the outburst. I reiterated that it wasn't our intent to offend him, assured them we'd communicate the agenda more clearly in the future, and emphasized how much we valued their time and partnership.

We worked hard to deliver a space that truly reflected the company's brand and culture. They loved the space they moved into a few months later and even expanded into a space across the street. The tough moments along the way brought us closer, and through the process, I became friends with one of the planning team members. It's a reminder that even in challenging situations, maintaining a positive attitude can lead to lasting friendships and successful outcomes.

When you find yourself in a situation that is negative or out of your control, watch for the small things that can set it back on course, and listen with an open mind to understand their point of view.

STARS GIVE BACK TO GO FORWARD

Bring your positive can-do attitude to an extracurricular activity that resonates with your soul. While your network of industry connections is now strong, standing out means developing relationships with the organizations that you are personally passionate about and using your platform to bring attention to those causes. For me, it was IIDA. I built a brand around that leadership role and demonstrated my ability to elevate an organization, give back to the community, and develop future leaders. This aligned deeply with my values.

If you are passionate about tree frogs in the Amazon or another cause, get involved in helping. Having a cause outside of work connects you to a wider community of people who are like-minded. Not only is this fulfilling, but it also shows people who you are.

There are organizations for every cause, but if you find yourself struggling and you don't know where to start, check out the organizations that your friends and colleagues are a part of. There may be something there that resonates with you. If not, it might be an opportunity to start something new.

STARS BUILD THE TEAM UP

Building community inside the firm is just as important as building community outside of the firm. If you are not connecting with a colleague, it is in your best interest and the best interest of the firm to solve the issue. From what I have seen, personality conflicts are put in our path to help us grow. Instead of complaining or thinking the person on the other side of the issue is difficult, find common ground. Demonstrate to your team that you care about them, your collective goals, and winning together.

When you go to HR with a personality conflict, it can reflect poorly on you. Instead, take the challenge to pull the person in as an ally. When I hired Chloe, she and Monica, the firm's senior interior designer, were like oil and water. Chloe tried to reach out to Monica and form a relationship, but nothing she tried worked. Frustrated, Chloe said in a matter-of-fact tone, "We are going to be friends." She took Monica (and me) completely by surprise, disarming Monica and putting it out there that Chloe was not going to give up, so Monica should just give in. It was funny, and it broke the ice. They worked well together after that, and I spied them at a few events actually enjoying each other's company.

STARS ARE DEALMAKERS

In our industry, a real estate broker typically is the first point of contact with a client. In the early days of looking for the right commercial space for the client, a broker might show them a dozen options. By the time they reach out to a design team, they are hoping that they can paint a vision for the client that will enable them to see themselves and their teams in that space. They are looking for you to close the deal.

Sometimes a space won't work, and it's our job to point something out that will help them narrow the search criteria and go back out to the market to find other options, but in my experience, a good designer can usually make the space work with clever planning. A designer who is a dealmaker will stand out and be on the broker's short list for future projects.

I overheard a broker on a call with a colleague. "Call James," he said. "He's a dealmaker." My ears perked up. That taught me how business can snowball just with one recommendation from the right person. Being a dealmaker resonates with brokers. It is a significant value-add to understand brokers' motivations and what is at risk for them if you fail to make a space work. In commercial real estate, this can be the difference between winning important work and being cut from the short list altogether.

STARS TAKE ACTION

My dad would always say, "Why do today what you can put off until tomorrow?" when he wanted me to know that I was being lazy. I am not lazy. But his point was always taken, and it motivated me to finish what I started. He constantly makes miracles happen. He is tenacious. When we needed a seawall built after a bad storm and erosion damage, every crew was booked solid for years out. We explored every avenue, even hiring engineers and builders across state lines to help. Of course, he found a crew willing to build a temporary wall that had the ability to get through permitting in the emergency situation we faced.

My dad taught me the value of getting done what needs to get done when I first learn it needs doing. I don't know if that's inherent in all New Englanders or just my family, but I find a lack of the same sense of urgency in some. Anyone looking to shoot to the top would have a deep advantage by folding in a sense of urgency and follow-through.

Urgency and effort are core to success. No matter the task, doing it efficiently and well will make you stand out. You will get more opportunities the more you demonstrate that you can handle the work well.

Putting other people's needs and concerns first—treating their meetings and deadlines as top priority—lets them know that you're part of their team. That you care about their project and work.

Action is important. Keep going!

LEVEL UP

Being a superstar in the design industry combines all you've learned and done so far and requires leveling it up to be more open and strategic with your actions. Your personal brand will be a reflection of the work you put in, the contacts you make, the work you win, and how people feel about working with you.

Your next goal is to form a core team to build synergy and deliver top-quality work together. At a minimum, aligning with a principal and job captain is essential, and over time, you'll add to your core team to enhance efficiency and effectiveness. Maintaining good relationships within this team will increase project profitability, enhance learning, and elevate your reputation as a collaborator and leader.

True star power is a combination of design skill, personality, and leadership acumen. If you're going to get to the top, developing your leadership skills is paramount to your success.

CHAPTER 12

LEARNING TO LEAD

I GOT AN EMAIL FROM EMMA IN RESPONSE TO A STERN message I'd sent out late the night before, assuming she had made a mistake on a design drawing. Emma and I had been working together for years. She knew that I welcomed pushback, and she knew that in this instance, she was right. "You're wrong about this," she said in her response to my message.

I went back to reread the message I'd sent and realized she *was* right—I was wrong. It was a full-circle moment for me. I now knew what Nina had felt all those years ago when she had reacted quickly to the missing files.

Everyone is fallible, even (and perhaps especially) leaders. One of the key jobs of a good leader is to create a safe environment for people to learn and sometimes fail as they develop. And that includes the leaders. When you trip, take a beat and see if there is anything you can learn from the situation. Apologize, and make any necessary repairs.

Emma and I have built a relationship based on trust and respect over years of working together. We have grace for each other when we need it and respect for what we each bring to the table. I push her, and she pushes me. Together we are part of a team dynamic that demonstrates a healthy working relationship to our peers.

Building a great team is a foundational step in being an effective leader. Whether you are part of a small team or leading a large department, putting the right people in the right place to do their best work is step one.

BUILD A GREAT TEAM

A good way to practice building a great team is by joining a board or committee through a professional organization. You will get to hone your skills in identifying and working with talent, motivating people under a unified vision, and delivering a tangible result—usually an event, piece of communications material, or fundraising goal rather than a client project.

My work with the IIDA New England board was essential in developing my skills for putting the right people together for a given project. Everyone on a committee brings unique talents and proficiencies to the table. They are also usually uniquely motivated, adding a layer of complexity to how you encourage them to work together. People don't generally get paid to be part of committees like this, so financial gain is not the incentive it might be at the office.

In my capacity as director of students, I led a committee of professors and design professionals who had been putting on Career Day for years before I arrived on the scene. The event had gone on hiatus before restarting the year I began. I quickly learned that the committee had good ideas, zero funding, and no one to help put ideas into action.

I ended up doing the lion's share of the legwork—securing a location, finding a sponsor to cover food and beverages, finding donors to supply the grand prize, designing and printing fliers, and getting busy professionals to hold the date on their calendars. The list was endless. By the final days leading up to the event, I was feeling a bit like the only one who had done anything at all to put this event together, and I was a little bitter about it. Then Career Day came, and as we opened the event, students poured in. The professors had made attendance a requirement, guaranteeing they would all show up. If we had not had their involvement, we would not have had a successful event. Everyone brings something to the table. Your job is to find out what it is and how it fits into the team dynamic.

Later, when I led IIDA New England as president, I found that my work as director of students came in handy, as it taught me to watch and listen for how the pieces of the puzzle came together. I looked at every position on the board, the work they had done to create value in their area, and their overall outlook on the year ahead. What I discovered was that everyone at the table was at a different place in their leadership journey. Some were eager to make change, and some were satisfied with the status quo.

As we set about crafting a vision for the future, the right people started falling into place, and the people who needed to move on were thanked for their hard work and encouraged to make space for new community members to learn and give back in the way they had for many years. It was a hard transition for some, but the life it breathed into the board gave us all energy to move forward in lockstep.

As you engage with a committee, you will learn what you are good at and what you need to practice. It may be the first time you have been able to run a budget, solicit quotes, or hire a service provider. These are important components to the operations side of running a firm as well. When you pick up these skills in committee work, you are getting the opportunity to learn and improve your process for the future.

You will also learn how to be part of and lead a team. You may get tasks at the office as part of a larger team, but on a committee, you may be asked to think ahead, anticipate what is coming next, and jump in to solve issues. This knowledge comes in handy when you start leading project work.

Your professional organization may also offer specific leadership training, such as an emerging or developing leaders group. The first year the Emerging Leaders program launched under IIDA New England, I recruited Sylvie to help create content and align resources to make it an outstanding program. Sylvie was a rep at the time and was well connected with the firms in the area. She put on wonderful events that were well attended and had worked for respected firms before jumping to the rep side of the business. Sylvie and I brainstormed on what classes we wished we had had when we were coming up in the industry.

Here is a sample of the training the Emerging Leaders received:

- 90-Minute MBA
- Understanding Tenant Markets
- Crafting a Story
- Communication
- Business Etiquette
- Public Speaking and Presenting
- Who's Who (identifying the difference between owners, project managers, brokers, construction managers, etc.)

We helped program participants craft their elevator pitch, went over how to build your personal brand, and had a seasoned business development expert from a local firm describe how firms built their networks, got work, did follow-up, and made lasting connections. (Psst: Her number-one tip was "Give before you get.")

Find opportunities to develop your abilities to build a team either inside or outside the office, and work on yourself to be a successful team member.

PROVIDE CONSTRUCTIVE CRITICISM

During my time as an instructor at the Boston Architectural College (BAC), I had the opportunity to teach studio and foundation courses and to learn how to be a better instructor from an amazing teacher of teachers, Tina Blythe. Tina was then the director of faculty development at the BAC, a lecturer at Harvard University, and an author of many books in her area of expertise. Her insights around teaching for understanding helped me to better connect with my students and improved my ability to provide constructive feedback.

While I taught classes two nights per week and on Saturdays, other instructors and I met with Tina one evening per week in an intensive session where she would guide us on how to teach to different personalities and learning styles, along with giving us incredible resources to further understand these concepts.

Part of our instruction was to practice how to interact with students. We'd role-play how to word various responses, and feedback to be encouraging and constructive instead of negative or punishing. I integrated the teaching skills into my class, and it was like magic as I watched it take effect on my students and their work.

Teaching is the art of how to meet people where they are, collaborate, communicate clearly, and motivate them effectively. You get immediate feedback when your communication is unclear and your metrics are too vague, as the results you get back on assignments demonstrate how effective you were in those areas. Small tweaks to how you communicate begin to build, and you can watch students excel before your eyes.

Students are developing, just like your teams, and everyone is at a different stage coming in. Not everyone will be a superstar—some may not even want to be—so you have to meet each person where they are and play to their strengths and overall goals. That's the basic role of any teacher, and arguably any leader.

Practicing what kind of feedback resonates and what falls flat is important as you develop your leadership skills. One way to practice articulating feedback is to participate in critiques at local universities. Just as your university may have done, teachers often reach out to firms with alumni who may be willing to come in and review student work. This gives the student an opportunity to present to a professional who hasn't been following along all semester and allows them to receive some real-world feedback.

I learned quickly how to give honest feedback without offending people, though I made some mistakes in the beginning. "That's ugly," or "That's not going to work" is much easier to say than a carefully constructed, "Have you thought about your client and what they would want in that space? Does this solution match the feeling they're going for?" or "Have you considered the color scheme? What does it say about the client and their party?"

One of my biggest failures came during a critique of a senior-level Commercial Design Studio. The previous instructor had resigned midyear, leaving the school in a bind. I jumped in to help fill in the gap until they could find a replacement for the next term.

The students were designing a hotel and had completed the layout, initial finish selections, and furniture options. With no rapport with the class, I dove in with a harsh critique. I had expectations that a senior class would be more developed and able to handle more direct feedback. I was wrong.

One student, in particular, pushed back hard on me, questioning my experience and making statements that I didn't have a right to critique their work based on likes or dislikes—that design was subjective. We ended the class on a contentious note, and the department head asked me to come in and talk about what had happened. I was sure I'd be asked to leave the class and not come back.

Instead, the department head asked me to try again with a little more patience and consideration for the work the students had done. I reevaluated my critique style, knowing I had been too harsh, and prepared to go in the following week. It was one of the hardest things I'd done as an instructor, as the students were understandably hostile toward me. I acknowledged their frustration and explained I wanted to help them improve and prepare them for the realities of the design world. I asked for their trust and patience, much as the department head had done for me. It was a turning point for me and for the class.

COMMUNICATE WITH AUTHORITY

One of the hardest things for young leaders to develop is their "voice." When I was teaching and then leading professional organizations, I was working on crafting a voice that was confident and encouraging but also authoritative.

When you're early in your career and you find yourself in a position of leadership, it's easy to question if you deserve to be there. You may second-guess your ideas or suggestions, but remember: you're in that position for a reason. Your experience and perspective are valuable.

To develop this authoritative voice, practice speaking up in meetings, offering your insights, and backing them up with well-researched points. It's about balancing confidence with humility, knowing when to assert your opinion and when to listen.

I found that public speaking courses, like the one from Toastmasters, helped immensely. Engaging in forums where you can practice speaking and receive feedback from peers or mentors is invaluable. It will feel uncomfortable at first, but with practice, you'll find your voice.

INTO THE WOODS

Reflecting on my journey through various leadership roles, it is clear that leading is less about having all the answers and more about fostering an environment where growth and collaboration can thrive. Whether through forming teams, providing constructive criticism, or cultivating a compelling vision, the essence of leadership lies in understanding and lifting those around you.

The experiences shared in this chapter underscore a fundamental truth: leadership is a continuous learning process. Each interaction, each mistake, and each success contributes to your evolution as a leader. Embrace these moments with humility and an open mind, always ready to adapt and grow.

In your path to becoming an effective leader, remember to build strong relationships, just as I have with Emma. Trust and respect are the cornerstones of any successful team. Engage with professional organizations to sharpen your skills and broaden your perspective. Provide thoughtful, constructive feedback that encourages development, and always communicate with clarity and confidence.

Leadership is not about perfection but about persistence, learning, and the willingness to improve. By fostering a supportive environment, staying true to your vision, and continuously honing your skills, you can inspire your team to achieve greatness and create meaningful, lasting impact.

CHAPTER 13

YOU MADE IT! NOW WHAT?

WHEN I LEFT BOSTON, PEOPLE WERE SHOCKED. THEY couldn't comprehend why I would leave a place where I was so deeply ingrained in the culture. One colleague who visited us in Portland said, "I am so confused; you were such a part of the industry. It makes no sense." But to me, it made perfect sense.

I didn't grow up with siblings. My baby daughter, Ava, was the first diaper I ever changed. At that time, I was leading exciting projects at Baker Design Group with a fantastic team. However, at home, Ed and I lacked family support. My parents were in Oregon and Maine, far from Massachusetts. Despite having a wonderful nanny and a supportive design community, I needed my mom. Balancing work and home life became increasingly difficult, and by the time my daughter started walking, I was truly struggling.

One night, after Ava was in bed and the nanny had left, I told my mom over the phone, "I wish you lived here." During her bedtime routine, I'd asked Ava to close the door as I settled into her big blue reading chair. She looked at me with confusion. I tried again, but still no response. On a hunch, I tried Spanish, the nanny's first language. Ava smiled and toddled over to close the door. At that moment, I realized something had to change if I wanted my daughter to be raised by me and not the nanny, but I wasn't sure what. I felt stuck.

Later that week, I discovered Tony Robbins was holding a seminar in West Palm Beach, coinciding with my planned visit to a friend there. It felt like a sign, so I registered immediately. For those unfamiliar, Tony Robbins is a prominent figure in the self-improvement space, an author of numerous books, and an inspirational motivator to millions.

Upon arriving in West Palm Beach, I contracted the flu. Despite feeling miserable, I attended the sessions, armed with cold medicine and a determination to figure myself out. The seminar, held in a massive convention center, seated thousands of people. Tony Robbins employs specific strategies to break patterns, including uncomfortable seats and freezing interior temperatures. Veteran attendees came prepared with winter jackets, hats, and pillows. I ended up buying a sweatshirt from the swag table in the lobby, having dressed for Florida, not Alaska.

Tony asked us to write down our goals in various areas of life. Starting with career and finances, I noted some obvious goals. They seemed straightforward, almost like foregone conclusions, and didn't excite me as they once had. Then he said, "Now write down your goals around family." I stared at my blank sheet of paper, paralyzed. Despite having a wonderful husband, an amazing daughter, and a great relationship with my parents, I felt like a total failure in this area. I was disconnected.

As if reading my mind, he said, "I feel sorry for the people who don't know what to write."

That's me! I thought.

He continued, "Finding out what you want has to be the first step."

It became clear that focusing on my family and being prepared to embrace a shift was essential to feel more connected to the people I loved. This realization was daunting—work was comfortable and rewarding—but it would require me to push myself and establish goals for my home life.

I flew back to Boston with a spark to act on my newfound revelation, and as if in protest against change, my eardrum burst. I still had the flu, and the cabin pressure from the plane built up in my ear. This physical pain, paired with the unknown road ahead, brought me to a new low.

A few weeks later, my mom visited and made everything seem easier. Her bond with Ava was obvious, and her care was just what we needed to heal. During that trip, she brought a copy of *Portland Monthly* magazine, featuring the best neighborhoods in Portland, with details on home prices, schools, and amenities. I began to imagine what it would be like to give Ava what I'd had—a grandma living one street over in a smaller city.

"Maybe we should just move to Portland," I suggested to Ed as I paged through the magazine the next morning.

He looked at me for a moment to gauge my seriousness and then said, "Let's do it."

I've always been a "go with your gut" person, so once I decided to move, there was no looking back. In two months, we were living on the West Coast.

From the outside, it looked like career suicide. However, it ended up being the best thing I could have done, giving me the ability to establish and reach both personal and professional goals. I joined the Portland team at IA and leveraged the techniques I had learned in Boston to grow a community in my new city. As luck would have it, Design Museum, an organization Ed and I had been connected with in Boston, was expanding to Portland at the time of our move. We got involved as part of the Advisory Council, helping to establish the Museum in Portland. The council was responsible for making introductions and ideating on exhibits that would be a good fit for the Portland community. It was just the opportunity I was looking for to meet people and talk about the power of design with like-minded individuals.

In spite of an initial pay cut, eventually, moving to Portland gave me more opportunities and more income than I had given up in Boston. I was able to launch my own firm and set a new vision for how a firm could collaborate and be successful. I have balance now. Not every day, but most days.

So ask yourself, when you're on track but still aren't feeling fulfilled, are you happy with what you are doing? Is work allowing you to fulfill your basic needs in life? It doesn't have to fulfill all of them in and of itself, but it has to allow each of those needs to be fulfilled elsewhere if necessary. Life is so much richer with those other aspects filled in.

You may not need to start over from scratch the way I did, but you should remain open to the best life possible. Follow your gut.

Assuming that you are leveraging the information here, one day you will be a top performer in your firm. You will inspire teams, hone your leadership skills, be involved in the community in a way that resonates with you, and establish a brand outside your firm that gives you flexibility as you continue to grow in your career.

Now that you made it, it's time to look at what is next.

WHAT ARE YOUR PRIMARY GOALS?

The power of clarity and focused intention cannot be overstated when talking about achieving your dreams. Let's say your intention is to lead a top 100 firm. Narrow your focus to a few firms, and really dig into the details of how each one operates. Who do you know who works there? What is the culture like? What types of projects do they do? Can you picture yourself working for a firm that size? When you get clear about what you want, you can chart a course to get there.

WHAT'S YOUR AREA OF EXPERTISE?

Becoming a subject matter expert (SME, pronounced smee) distinguishes you in a firm. Choosing an area that is trending may get you good press. For example, if you are interested in sustainable design, you might consider becoming an expert in cross-laminated timber (CLT). Or if you are interested in workplace design, you may consider becoming an expert in which types of office conversion projects are working and which are not.

There is an incredible range of areas of expertise in design and architecture. Wherever your passion lies will be the easiest for you to devote the time, energy, and growth required to do it well. Pick one or two, and make yourself the go-to person for that specialty. You can also choose to be a generalist; however, putting your focus into the area you are most passionate about will make for a happier and more successful work experience.

WHAT DO YOU WANT TO BE PAID?

One time, I was asked to get a file out of a coworker's pedestal file cabinet. I opened the drawer and saw her paycheck, which was more than I ever thought was possible for a senior designer. It opened my mind to what was possible and gave me a higher earning goal.

Money isn't the most important thing, but it shouldn't be ignored either. Having a goal can give you insight into whether you will need to start your own firm or if you are comfortable working for someone else for your career. There is no right or wrong answer.

People often choose to work for someone else to have more stability; however, in my experience, the cash flow of a firm follows a cycle, and you are no more stable at a job where you work for someone else than you would be if you worked for yourself. Since we design buildings, our work starts and ends, and we work to keep the pipeline full of opportunities so that when one job ends, another is sliding into its place. This isn't a guarantee for any of us, and if you find that you are a rainmaker, you may find yourself wondering one day why you are doing it for someone else rather than yourself.

HOW DO YOU CONTINUE TO GROW?

Asking for feedback helps you discover what works and what doesn't as you grow into a leader. Applying what you learn establishes trust with your team. Look for ways to grow, from reading about new techniques to attending conferences in your area of expertise. The industry is always changing, so staying sharp on your industry knowledge, leadership skills, and design skills is an important part of serving your team and clients to the best of your ability.

The more senior you become, the more challenging it can be to carve out time for reflection and growth. Making these priorities will help you to maintain your focus on your goals and fold in new ones as you learn more about the type of leader you want to become.

SHOULD YOU STAY OR SHOULD YOU GO?

One look at my LinkedIn profile and you can see that I have been at a wide range of firms. From small to large and everything in between, I felt like Goldilocks trying to find the perfect fit. Looking back, I wouldn't trade those moves for anything. I learned the lessons I am sharing with you here and met amazing people at each stop on my journey.

Designers in this industry have options. Many designers eventually leave firms to become material reps, owners' project managers, contractors, developers, or furniture specialists. Their time at design firms helps inform their new roles and gives them unique perspectives.

If you are frustrated with your current situation or having a difficult time getting a job, maybe the universe is pushing you in a new direction that will be more fulfilling—and potentially more profitable. Assess your options, and follow your gut.

When I started Thunder Egg, I was creating my perfect fit. I envisioned a firm of talented, ego-free designers working with clients who were changing the world for the better. What I got was a group of entrepreneurial, heart-forward professionals with whom I love collaborating every day. As a leader, my job is to create the best work environment for my team. This means alleviating roadblocks, allowing people to pick their rates and projects, and mentoring the people along the way. Our team's balance makes them more creative and happier, which our clients notice. We've built a reputation for quality, creativity, and reliability, and new clients often come to us through recommendations. I found a balance that works for me and a team that shares my ethos.

Finding your place in the design industry can be challenging, but it's worth it. Whether you choose to stay in a firm or explore new opportunities in adjacent fields, each step builds toward something great. Trust your journey. Find your perfect fit, and enjoy the ride.

ROOTS AND WINGS

I set the playlist and arranged glasses as my mother helped me clean up the yard and set up the lawn furniture for our Thunder Egg summer party. My mother joined us as our team and their families enjoyed delicious food, celebrated our wins, discussed future plans, and connected as friends. As my daughter played with the other kids and we savored the last drops of our rosé, I felt deeply grateful for the community we created and the bright future ahead.

The week after, we headed to Maine to visit my dad. While we talk almost daily, our family looks forward to our time on the East Coast catching up with family and friends. We've achieved a balance that isn't limited by geography, allowing us to maintain close family ties while pursuing our professional dreams.

My firm is thriving, taking on both national and international projects. We design spaces that resonate with the community, collaborating with teams and clients who share our vision for thoughtful, impactful design. The decision to leave Boston for Portland was transformative, bringing me closer to my family and enabling both personal and professional success. Having taken this leap of faith, we are confident that whatever the future holds, it will be bright.

Trust your instincts, and stay open to what's next. Your best life is waiting.

CONCLUSION

WHEN I LEFT BOSTON, I ASKED A COLLEAGUE IF THERE WAS anything I could do to help her. I suggested options: insider tips on firms, negotiation strategies, compensation advice. But she said, "Give me your Rolodex." For those under forty, that's a paper contact list of all the people you know. She understood. A robust network is the difference between surviving and thriving in your career. If you are doing it right, everyone you meet will help you or need your help sometime in your career.

The real story behind the curtain of the design industry is the relationships. To thrive in the first five years of your design career and beyond, you have to understand the ecosystem of the industry—how people are connected and how to connect people. That comes down to a few things.

Building your brand and the community that will carry you through your early career starts before you even interview. Don't be afraid to approach people to ask questions; they want to help you like others helped them.

It's not about you; it's about your firm. Find ways you can contribute to the success of the company. Once you realize you're part of a team, part of the greater good of the firm, then things will start clicking into place. More can be accomplished together than apart, and everything you put out into the world to help others will come back to you later.

How and why you join a firm and stay with a firm depends a lot on its culture and what opportunities that culture gives you to build your brand and contribute in meaningful ways. Do your research beforehand to find a good fit. For example, if equity is important to you, look for a firm with diverse staff and leadership. If you get into the firm and find out it isn't a good fit, you'll now have the knowledge to make a better choice for yourself and the increased experience to help you move to that better spot.

There's a large cast of industry characters involved in creating a building. Know who they are and what motivates them. Understand where you are in the industry ecosystem, and carve out your niche. Make friends with everyone. They'll help you find work or move firms, and they'll go to bat for you if you're in a pinch, hoping you'll do the same for them.

Those authentic connections will form friendships that can last a lifetime. Align yourself with people who share your values and goals and who will cheer you on along the way. Your reputation is part of your brand, so make sure it aligns with who you are and what you stand for.

Take the good with the bad. Even a toxic situation can be used for good if it helps you learn what *not* to do as a leader, solidifies your values, and pushes you towards your best self.

Mentors are essential. Learning is not done in a vacuum. Are there people out there doing what you are doing? Who can guide you over the important stepping stones in your career, both professional and personal? Assess your knowledge gaps. Understand what you need, and ask for it politely. Then be open to feedback. They may not be perfect all the time, but they want to help you. And they can, sometimes from the other side of the world if need be, and they are helpful resources when things change and new skill sets are needed.

Stars are sought after by both firms and clients because they help others achieve their goals. A job well done helps others do their jobs well. If you hold tight to that intention, you're sure to shine.

Seek opportunities to round out your skill sets through safe leadership roles that allow you to make mistakes and practice in low-stakes environments. Not everyone wants to lead, but even if you want to be a detailing expert for the rest of your career, you can still grow to your fullest extent within that role.

Be open to the next step. You'll never have a final iteration as long as you keep growing. Run your own race, and don't compare your finish line with others'. The contributions and achievements that make you happy will be different for everyone.

Should you be in this profession? Maybe; maybe not. Now that you know what it takes to succeed, you know that it isn't for everyone. Maybe being a designer isn't the final stop on your career path. Maybe you will go into sales, furniture design, or procurement or be an owner's representative or move into another adjacent field. All that matters is that you don't give up on your dream.

We get into design because it's a passion. We shape how people move through the world. That's important work. Doing our best at that work means understanding the relationships that create those opportunities. That's why I wanted to write this book. I saw too many talented designers stumble on the soft skills required to succeed in this industry, and I'm hoping these insights will give today's designers the knowledge they need to thrive and to build a better tomorrow for our industry.

To move forward in your design career, have a clear vision of where you want to go. Learn from the paths others have paved. This journey takes time, so keep pushing through even when it gets tough. Cry if you need to. Work out. Talk to friends. Hold your boundaries while continuing to grow professionally. Make mistakes—that's the only way to truly learn and thrive.

This is your chance to be brave.

To learn more, join our community at BrittneyHerrera.com. Let me know what I missed in this book or what you'd like to learn more about. Drop me a line on LinkedIn or via email to say hello. I can't meet everyone for coffee—not that it wouldn't be nice—but I'm here to support you as you grow.

ACKNOWLEDGMENTS

FIRST AND FOREMOST, I WANT TO EXPRESS MY DEEPEST gratitude to my family, the unwavering foundation of support behind this book.

To my husband, Ed, thank you for being my sounding board and for cheering me on through every challenge. I eagerly anticipate writing the next chapter of our story together.

To my daughter, Ava, your smile lights up the world. Thank you for teaching me to live in the moment while pursuing my dreams.

To my parents, Terry and Darrell, your hard work and integrity have shown me the value of leaving the world better than we found it. Your influence is a gift I carry with me daily.

To the Scribe family—Amanda, Ellie, Emily, Ami, and Anna— thank you for your dedication to supporting this book. Your meticulous attention to every word and detail, along with your guidance through each iteration, has been invaluable. Your work in keeping the reader at the forefront of my mind through every twist and turn is deeply appreciated.

To my mentors, this book reflects your collective investment in my growth. Your teaching, guidance, corrections, and leadership have been instrumental. I am profoundly grateful for your wisdom and support. Special thanks to Lisa Killaby, Angela Juliano, and Jeff Tompkins for their profound mentorship. Each of you has taught me more than I could ever capture here. I appreciate your leadership, example, and impact on the next generation.

And to you, the reader, I believe in your potential and dreams. May this book be a beacon that lights your path and empowers you to achieve all you aspire to.

ABOUT THE AUTHOR

BRITTNEY HERRERA, IIDA, LEED AP, is the founder and creative director of Thunder Egg. With a career spanning top design firms like Gensler, IA, and SGA, she has led projects for clients including Tripadvisor, Amazon, and adidas. Brittney is an NCIDQ-certified interior designer, past president of the IIDA New England Chapter, and former professor at the Boston Architectural College. Her accolades include the Portland *Daily Journal of Commerce*'s Phenom Award and the IIDA Leadership Award. An alumna of Rochester Institute of Technology, Brittney mentors future design leaders and shapes environments for global brands across international markets. You can find her community at BrittneyHerrera.com.